HOW TO
USE PEOPLE
TO
GET WHAT YOU WANT
AND STILL BE A
NICE GUY!

HOW TO
USE PEOPLE
TO
GET WHAT
YOU WANT
AND STILL BE A
NICE GUY!

A GUIDE TO NETWORKING KNOW-HOW

LES GARNAS

PETERSON'S
PRINCETON, NEW JERSEY

Library of Congress Cataloging-in-Publication Data
Garnas, Les.
    How to use people to get what you want and still be a nice guy /
Les Garnas.
        p.   cm.
    Includes index.
    ISBN 1-56079-336-8 : $12.95
    1. Success in business—United States.   2. Businessmen—Social
networks—United States.   3. Social networks—United States.   I.
Title
HF5386.G217   1994
650.1'3—dc20   94-21840
                                                                       CIP

Cover design: Greg Wuttke

Interior design: CDS Designs

Printed in the United States of America

10 9 8 7 6 5 4 3 2 1

DEDICATION

To Carole, Barbara and Jeff: Thanks for willingly supporting my dreams, and for your patience in waiting for outcomes.

CONTENTS

INTRODUCTION

Whether you realize it or not, you're probably networking constantly in both your professional and personal lives. You call business acquaintances to tell them about job opportunities you think they'd be right for. You're at an industry conference and meet a colleague from another state whom you plan to keep in touch with. Your neighbor tells you about a possible lead for your business.

And whether you realize it or not, you *need* to network constantly to be successful in meeting the challenges of today's tough business climate. As companies continue to downsize, you need every tool you can get to thrive—and perhaps survive—in your job. With the American work force becoming more mobile, you want to know people who can help you with your next career move. If you're one of the millions of Americans who have started their own businesses, you always have to be looking for your next client.

I want to introduce you to a totally new way of thinking about networking. Successful networking is a never-ending process that is always changing and shifting, expanding and contracting, growing and maturing. It's an activity that focuses on building long-term relationships that provide benefits for everyone involved. It's an important business skill that enhances your effectiveness in your job or profession and helps you to further your career. And it's an enjoyable experience that can also yield benefits in your personal life.

I'm not promising you any miracles. There's no magic. No instant results. What I *am* offering in this book are common sense techniques that have worked splendidly for me over the past 25 years as I've made my way in corporations, professional partnerships, and my own business.

Here's a preview of what you can learn from this book:

- Techniques to help you build capital so that you can stack the deck in favor of success in your job, career, business, and personal life.
- The qualities that differentiate successful networkers from the rest.
- Where, when, and with whom to network.
- The importance of reciprocity, the cornerstone of good networking.
- How to develop your own style, adapting the networking process to your own unique personality.

In preparing this book, I've drawn from my own networking experiences as well as those of my many networking partners. I'd like to thank those partners for all the valuable lessons they taught me. Bruce Marcus also deserves kudos for his insight into networking style and his uncanny ability to help me communicate complex concepts simply so that you can identify with the process and make it your own. I want to acknowledge Dr. Deborah Tannen, professor of linguistics at Georgetown University, whose research has helped me understand differences in the natural networking styles of men and women and how each can benefit from the other's approach. Thanks, too, to Susan Camardo, a business writer and corporate communications consultant, for her assistance in helping me to put it all together.

One last word: As you read this book and apply its principles, don't forget that networking can and should be *fun*. And if you have as much fun as I've had, you're in for a great adventure. Good luck!

WHAT'S IT
ALL ABOUT

What is Networking? A Fresh Perspective

Networking (net' wurk-ing) *n.* 1. The consistent application of interpersonal skills in cultivating individuals for mutual benefit and lasting relationships. 2. A process that everyone, regardless of personality type, line of business, or level of experience, can use to enrich their professional and personal lives.

I hope this definition comes as a surprise to you because it's a very different way of thinking about networking than most people are accustomed to. Many individuals perceive networking as simply making acquaintances over pleasant conversation at a conference or social gathering. Others limit networking to an exchange of business cards followed by vague promises to keep in touch. And a lot of people leave it to chance, haphazardly responding to immediate opportunities that fall into their laps. But each of these is a very constricted view of what networking can be. So get ready to broaden your horizons and reap the rewards of your new, expanded perception of networking.

1. NETWORKING IS THE CONSISTENT APPLICATION OF INTERPERSONAL SKILLS IN CULTIVATING INDIVIDUALS FOR MUTUAL BENEFIT AND LASTING RELATIONSHIPS.

The consistent application of interpersonal skills means how you treat people over time—how you communicate with them, how you behave toward them, how you support them. It involves both content and style—*what* you say and do, and *how* you say and do it. Because "interpersonal," by definition, describes relations between people, these skills include listening to what others say and responding with words and actions appropriate to the needs and preferences they express.

In using your interpersonal skills to cultivate others, the goal you're working toward is *mutual benefit*. Networking is all about reciprocity—doing for others as they do for you. This is the single most important element of a good networking relationship, yet the one that is most often misunderstood. Ignoring it can doom the most energetic networking efforts to failure.

Let's face it, we're all motivated by self-interest. You engage in networking because you want something out of it—a lead to a new job or a new client, for example. And the people you're dealing with want something, too. They're naturally asking themselves, "What's in this for me?" Put yourself in their position for a moment—a good place to be, since networking works both ways and you'll also be on the receiving end of requests for help. Taking some action on behalf of another takes time and attention away from your own priorities. If you feel you'll get something of value back, you're more likely to want to make the effort. This doesn't mean that the payback has to come immediately. Often, you or the person you're networking with will make an investment by doing something now in expectation of the courtesy being returned in the future. But the point is, there eventually has to be a payback for both parties.

What Networking Is
Cultivating others for mutual benefit Remembering to reciprocate Developing sustaining relationships Making connections, instead of contacts Useful in your personal as well as professional life A skill that everyone can learn

So the essence of a mutual benefit orientation is developing a trusting, giving relationship with another for individual gain, yet overall mutual benefit. That brings us to another important component of networking: building lasting relationships. The most successful networking situations are those in which you create a long-term partnership with someone who can help you achieve your objectives.

The way you develop these sustaining relationships is by making connections, not just contacts. Making connections means getting to know your partners at a level deeper than superficial awareness. It means being sensitive enough to be able to walk in their shoes, caring about things that concern them, wanting to help them achieve and celebrate successes, understanding their needs, playing into their strengths, recognizing their weaknesses, and finding ways to help complement their goals. Think of the kind of connection you have with your friends and family—you keep in close and constant touch with them and find ways to reciprocate favors. I'm not saying that your networking relationships will—or should—develop to the same degree of intimacy. But this is the model when it comes to cultivating your networking partners.

Obviously, you can't have this depth of relationship with everyone you meet. So as you consciously expand your circle of business and social acquaintances, be discerning in choosing those people with whom you'd like to develop a lasting networking partnership.

You may have pleasant contacts with many people who pass in and out of your life, from your hairdresser to your office building's newsstand operator to your local service station owner. But because there's no mutual benefit in cultivating them, they need to be differentiated from those people who do, or could, have an important influence on your life.

So who are the kinds of people you want to cultivate? Your choices depend on your personal networking goals. Here are a few examples. If you're looking for a job, you want to connect with people who are familiar with what's happening in your line of work and can recommend you to others in your field. If you have your own business, or you're a doctor, lawyer, accountant, or other professional whose livelihood depends on attracting new clients, make a point of getting to know people who are in a position to give you business. If you want to be more effective within your organization, it helps to cultivate influential individuals inside the company—up, down, and across departmental or divisional lines—for support and mutual benefit.

What Networking Isn't

One-sided manipulation of another person
Pleasant social conversation with no specific purpose in mind
Restricted to powerful, aggressive, or well-connected people
A matter of luck or chance

No matter what your immediate purpose in networking, the solid and sustaining relationships you develop can continue to be mutually advantageous in other situations as the needs and goals of both you and your partners change. But in all the networking connections you make, never forget the Golden Rule of Reciprocity: Do for others as they do for you.

2. NETWORKING IS A PROCESS THAT EVERYONE, REGARDLESS OF PERSONALITY TYPE, LINE OF BUSINESS, OR LEVEL OF EXPERIENCE, CAN USE TO ENRICH THEIR PROFESSIONAL AND PERSONAL LIVES.

Since the concept of networking is often associated with high-visibility movers and shakers, you might mistakenly think that only a select group of outgoing, dynamic business and political leaders who travel in the rarefied circles of other powerful people own the monopoly on successful networking. Not true. It's important to understand that networking is something that *anyone*—and that means you—can use to help get what he or she wants out of life. It's not knowledge that you're born with or something that only comes naturally to people with outgoing or aggressive temperaments. Once you learn the process and practice it over time, networking becomes a skill you can apply in any situation you choose. To enjoy at least modest success, all you need is a goal, some measure of patience, and a moderate commitment. Beyond that, the sky's the limit—the degree of success you get out of networking is directly related to the amount of energy you put into it.

When most people talk about networking, they tend to think in terms of furthering their jobs or careers. Certainly that's a big part of it, and I'll be focusing primarily on the business applications of networking throughout this book. But once you learn how to network effectively, you'll find that it can be useful in other areas of your life as well, including social situations, political activities, and making a contribution to your community. I'll be giving you examples of how you can use networking to enhance your personal life in later chapters. In the meantime, keep this expanded definition of networking in mind as you read on so that you can start applying the good networking habits you learn to everything you do.

DOS AND DON'TS

Do: Broaden your perception of what networking is and how it can work for you.

Do: Look for mutual benefit in all of your networking exchanges.

Do: Develop trusting, long-term relationships with your networking partners.

Don't: Think that networking is limited to people with certain personalities or experiences—it's for everyone.

Don't: Expect to develop networking relationships with everyone you meet—choose wisely.

Don't: Forget the Golden Rule of Reciprocity: Do for others as they do for you.

So Why Network?
Building Capital

The more you think about the definition of networking I suggested in the last chapter, the more you'll realize that networking can yield far more benefits than you may ever have imagined. When you make a long-term investment in the people you choose to network with, you're setting up a networking bank account. You make deposits by helping your networking partners to accomplish their goals. In return, you can make withdrawals by asking them to help you get what you need or value.

Think of this process as building capital. Through cultivating networking partners for mutual benefit, you have access to a wealth of assets and advantages that allow you to influence situations and events that are important to you. And you can draw from this savings account by calling on your partners for assistance in making decisions or setting priorities, dealing with sensitive issues, pursuing job opportunities or career directions, and exploring options and windows of opportuntity. Let me show you how it works.

Building Your Job Capital

Every organization—be it a corporation, law firm, school, hospital, small business, or whatever—needs skilled, responsible employ-

Set Up Networking Bank Accounts for . . .
Your Job Your Career Your Business Your Personal Life

ees to help it meet the challenges of the next century. All around us we're seeing a seismic shift in the way America does business. Companies that downsized during the recession continue to operate with fewer employees. The move toward a global economy is putting added pressure on corporations to compete on a worldwide scale. In this new environment, organizations are placing a high value on teamwork. Not only are they setting up functional teams dedicated to particular tasks, but they also prize interdepartmental cooperation that saves time, money, and energy. They want employees who are dedicated to working toward larger company goals.

This is good news for you as a networker because it provides a golden opportunity to use your networking skills to be perceived as a valuable employee. Networking in the workplace is a defined and focused activity in which you and your partners help one another to enhance your job performance, gain recognition, and be successful in a sharply competitive business environment. In the process, you usually help the company as well. And that can increase your chances of being favorably noticed by management.

I'll give you specific tips about on-the-job networking in the chapter called "Up, Down, and Across the Organization." But generally, it involves making connections with people throughout the company, especially in other departments you have frequent contact with. By establishing a networking bank account with these partners, you can find many ways to benefit yourselves and the company—for example, by getting work done more quickly and easily, by creating new systems to save time and money, and by improving communication and morale.

Let's look at how Carl, a purchasing manager for a large electronics manufacturer, used networking to cut costs and raise productivity in his company—and, as a result, saw his stock rise in the eyes of management.

> Carl works closely with research engineers who develop new product models; when successful prototypes become mainstream products, he purchases the components necessary for production. After he'd been on the job for a couple of months, Carl realized that better communication between purchasing and engineering would lead to more cost-effective product designs, so he came up with the idea of creating project teams. After getting the go-ahead from his boss to give it a try, he networked with the engineers over lunch, during breaks, and in the course of doing business, all the while explaining the benefits of his team concept and generating their support for his idea.
>
> After forming the teams with selected engineers he felt most comfortable with, Carl found that the relationship between the two groups improved by leaps and bounds. He became more creative in helping the engineers achieve their goals, and the engineers became more realistic about designing products that were cheaper and easier to produce.
>
> Carl also networked with other purchasing managers by sharing his team model with them and suggesting ways that they could implement it themselves, thus winning the support of his peers. He also networked with management by providing periodic progress reports to his department head as well as supervisors in the engineering department, explaining how the team concept was getting results in terms of more efficient use of time and improved morale. Soon, senior managers in purchasing and engineering began discussing the team approach and its results with top management and eventually everyone became aware of how Carl's efforts were helping the company prosper.

Carl created widespread appreciation for his job performance by using networking to build the support he needed to make his team concept a reality and thereby improve the output of both the engineering and purchasing departments. Could he have gained a reputation as a valued employee through traditional means—the faithful pursuit of his job as outlined by a job description? Perhaps. But this would have left the company's perception of his value much more to chance. Carl succeeded by stepping out of the job description box and taking responsibility for helping the company succeed. His awareness of the company's needs and priorities and his dedication to finding ways to make a contribution earned him the esteem of both his peers and top management.

By using networking to enhance your job—to get things done more creatively, efficiently, and effectively—you can build a lot of job capital to draw on in the future, especially in two areas that are of great concern to every employee: keeping your job and getting promoted. When a company downsizes and managers have to decide which staff members to cut, those employees with a recognized value will usually survive. It's to your advantage to be considered a sterling asset so that those who are making personnel decisions view you as being important to the future success of the department where you work and even to the organization as a whole. At one time, this might have been viewed as playing the game of corporate politics. But today, just being a good politician or a good soldier is no longer enough. While I can't say that networking will guarantee that you keep your job, I do believe that applying the principles of good networking within your company gives you more control over your destiny.

Smart networking within your organization can also pay a dividend by bringing you to the attention of managers who hold the keys to promotion. A visible and valuable employee who is widely known and respected throughout the company by both peers and managers is a likely candidate for a position of more responsibility and authority.

Building Job Capital Pays Off

Dan and Marisa are editorial assistants in the public relations department of a nonprofit organization. Budget cuts dictate that one of them has to go. Both are smart and competent. Dan has responded faithfully to whatever requests the boss has made. Marisa has done that and more. Realizing that public relations work often requires getting immediate and accurate information, she's gone out of her way to cultivate people in other areas of the organization who are in a position to give her the facts and figures she needs when she needs them. If you were the head of the department, who would you keep?

One note of caution as you network beyond your immediate area to increase your job capital: Always keep your boss aware of what you're doing outside of your department. You don't want to put him or her in the embarrassing situation of hearing about your activities from others, which makes it look as if he or she isn't on top of what's happening in the department. Your boss might then lose trust in you and perhaps even perceive you as threatening his or her job or violating the chain of command. It's up to you whether you write up a report on what you're doing or simply mention it in conversation. Just make sure to do it.

BUILDING CAPITAL FOR YOUR CAREER

Just as you can keep your savings account at the same bank even if you change your address, the career capital you accumulate over time stays with you from job to job. In fact, it comes in very handy when you're looking for a new position. If you stay in touch with the networking partners you make in each job even after you've left a position or company, over time you'll create a wide circle of influence. Since many of your partners will themselves move into new jobs, companies, and even industries, your networking reach continues to expand on its own momentum and you have lots more assets to draw on.

In developing and maintaining your career capital, you can also use some of your job capital to seed relationships in your own industry or in any other in which you see opportunity for your career over the long term. First, you want to establish a good reputation within your current job and company as a springboard to help you broaden your networking circle. When you're ready to extend your sphere of influence, move into the mainstream of your industry. Joining industry associations that depend on member synergy for many of their programs and initiatives is a smart move.

Trade on your corporate reputation to get onto key committees, work groups, panels, and speaker pools where you can work shoulder-to-shoulder with the movers and shakers of your industry. Associating with these prominent people boosts your image in the eyes of the group's members as well as in the industry at large. (See Appendix for names and addresses of key industry groups and associations.) Through your work on such committees, you can build a reputation for involvement, and perhaps even leadership, which will broaden awareness of who you are, what you're good at, and how vital you are in the industry.

This kind of visibility can yield double benefits for you. It plays well when decision makers are looking for the right person to represent their group—by speaking at a conference or running for office, for example—and see you as a viable candidate. And it's also likely to play well with your employer. If word gets back to your supervisors (through their own contacts) that you're highly valued in the industry, your company will look good for having you, and your value to your company could increase. In fact, developing industry capital can lead to promotions, higher visibility, and more respect within your own company. Just remember, though, to keep your boss informed of your industry activities. As we discussed in building job capital, you want your success to reflect well on, and be supported by, your boss, rather than be a source of tension or problems between you.

If you're in the market for a new job, the career capital you've built up is there to be drawn upon. Whether you are still employed or have already left your job, working your industry network will be a natural extension of your usual activities, not a big, new, and overwhelming task you have to perform. When you've already made connections with people who trust and respect you, you've done a good deal of the groundwork necessary to land yourself a great position.

BUILDING YOUR BUSINESS CAPITAL

Anyone whose livelihood depends on constantly bringing in new clients—from doctors and lawyers in a practice to salespeople and real estate agents on commission to entrepreneurs running their own companies—can use networking effectively to build business capital among a wide range of professional connections. For those of you who generate your own income, cultivating other businesspeople in many different industries and situations expands the potential for getting more work for your firm. The more creative you are in identifying and making connections with and among these networking partners, the more business capital you accrue for yourself.

Take the situation of Andrea, a commissioned salesperson of a large regional office furniture dealer. Andrea gets referred to many prospects by rental agents, architects, and interior designers, and in return recommends these sources to her clients or prospects who might need their services. She expanded her networking reach even further by producing a simple two-page monthly newsletter for clients and referral contacts that provides articles and listings of interest to both groups.

While putting together the newsletter represented a major invest-ment of time and energy, it gave Andrea a unique presence in the marketplace and clearly separated her from other sales representa-tives in her field. Over time, her hard work and multifaceted networking approach paid off handsomely in new clients and frequent referrals. It also put her and the line she represents at the forefront of the industry. She developed a reputation for being well-connected in the business community and is regarded as an intimate business advisor to her networking partners.

The synergistic potential for referral among businesspeople has made *some* avid networkers millionaires several times over. Many of today's multibillion-dollar companies started as one person's vision of a business built on a good product or service concept, combined with good networking skills with bankers, lawyers, and other businesspeople who could help these young companies grow. There's a common thread running from legendary industry giants such as James Cash Penney, Arthur Andersen, and Henry Ford to more contemporary entrepreneurs like Anita Roddick, Stephen Jobs, and Bill Gates. All made it a point to get to know people who were in a position to give them business, help them get money when their operations were starting out, and expand their influence as they prospered. Each had a vision, a plan, and the stick-to-it attitude to be successful personally and to make others successful as a reward for their involvement.

BUILDING CAPITAL IN YOUR PERSONAL LIFE

As you consider the benefits of networking, don't forget to set up an account for your personal life. In these situations, you're seeking to create capital for personal recognition, social acceptance, or support for a cause. This kind of networking is usually more casual than business networking and is based more on chance meetings and mutual interests rather than focused on specific results. But even in a nonprofessional setting, the rules of good networking still apply:

You have to deliver on the promise of mutual benefit for your partners, and draw on your skills, talents, and connections to help them just as they help you.

Leveraging Assets in Your Personal Life

For years, Glenn has been trying to get on the Board of Trustees of his city's Philharmonic orchestra, but it's a prestigious position and competition is stiff. When he hears that a board member is retiring at the end of the year, he goes into action. He shows the board roster to his networking connections to see if any of them knows someone on the list. It turns out that Margaret, his lawyer, used to work in the same firm as one of the trustees. Glenn explains to Margaret how his creative ideas and energy would help the board with important initiatives and then asks her to introduce him to the board member. What's in it for Margaret? She knows that Glenn will bring a fresh perspective and energetic participation to the board. And she'll look good for having referred him.

Here are some areas in which you can draw on your networking assets to help you achieve something you value in your personal life:

- *Social rewards.* Networking can help you identify and cultivate people who can sponsor your membership in clubs, nominate you to committees or boards you'd like to serve on, or get you invited to events you'd like to attend.
- *Community causes.* If you're active in charitable work, social causes, or a community project, you can call on your networking partners to make financial donations or in-kind contributions (giving products instead of money), to sign petitions or write letters, or to volunteer their professional services to a good cause.

■ *Political influence.* While politics is a very tricky area that needs to be handled delicately, you may want to enlist some like-minded networking partners in supporting a candidate for office—maybe even yourself!—or campaigning for changes in local, state, or national laws and policies that are important to you.

Where do you meet the people who will become your networking partners in your personal life? Everywhere you go outside of work—and sometimes inside as well. (For specific suggestions, see the chapter on "Making Connections.") Your personal and professional networking circles will often overlap as you discover areas of affinity that affect both business and pleasure.

You're definitely not going to expand your networking base sitting around waiting for someone to come knocking on your door. You have to get out there and become actively involved in meeting all types of people through all types of activities. In addition to making networking connections with people you might not ordinarily have a chance to meet, you'll find that putting time and energy into activities you care about can be greatly rewarding. And there's one more possible payoff: becoming involved, known, and respected in your community can build self-esteem and a sense of contribution that gives added meaning and dimension to your life.

DOS AND DON'TS

Do: Keep making deposits in your networking bank account to create plenty of credit with your partners.

Do: Use your networking skills to enhance your reputation as a valuable employee.

Do: Make sure your boss is aware of what you're doing outside of the department and the company.

Do: Use the career capital you accumulate over the years to broaden your circle of influence.

Do: Generate a wide range of professional connections to get more work for your business.

Do: Use networking in your personal life for social rewards, community causes, and political influence.

Don't: Make so many withdrawals from your networking accounts that you bankrupt your relationships.

Don't: Limit on-the-job networking to the people in your department.

Don't: Perceive networking as another form of corporate politics.

Don't: Lose touch with networking partners you make on the job when one of you moves on.

Don't: Overlook any opportunity to make networking connections in your personal life.

What Makes a Good Networker: Qualities + Actions = Results

True or False:

 a) **Successful networkers are aggressive and pushy.**
 b) **People who practice networking are usually manipulative.**
 c) **Networkers are "takers," not "givers."**

You've probably figured out already that if you answered "True" to any of these statements, it's time to think again about who all these people running around networking are. Actually, they're nice, normal people like you and me who are simply very savvy about how to make connections with other nice, normal people.

Throughout this chapter, I'll be exploring these three commonly held myths about networkers and explaining why the correct answer is "False." But now, let's look at the flip side and accentuate the positive—just what does make a person a good networker?

The Qualities of a Good Networker

As with everything else in life, there is no one hard-and-fast set of rules that guarantees success. But in my years as a dedicated networker who's always looking for my next partner, I've observed that successful networkers have a number of qualities in common. These aren't necessarily qualities that they—or you—were born with. They are positive traits that anyone can develop and apply to his or her networking plans and activities. And as you think about these attributes, remember that networking is a reciprocal process— just as you want to cultivate these qualities in yourself so that you stand out as someone desirable to be networked with, you also want to see them in your networking partners.

The Qualities of a Good Networker

Commitment
Curiosity
Perceptiveness
Good listener
Trusting and trustworthy
Goal-oriented
Strategic thinking
Focused yet flexible

Commitment

To be a successful networker, you have to be sincerely dedicated to making the process work for you. You have to be willing to take the time and make the effort required to get results. This means having the discipline to carry on with your networking activities when life gets hectic and you'd rather be doing something else, the patience to stick with it even if it takes awhile for your efforts to bear fruit, and the faith that the networking process will help you get what you want.

Curiosity

Being genuinely curious—really wanting to know about other people and what they do and think—stands a networker in good stead. It propels you to learn and grow and expand your horizons because you're always exploring something new. It makes meeting people easy and natural since you're asking questions of your potential partner that you truly want to know the answers to. You gain a lot of useful information about the other person that will be helpful as you develop your networking relationship and look for ways to help each other out. Seasoned networkers know that potential partners who are curious will always be looking for opportunity—for themselves as well as for their networking partners.

Perceptiveness

Having a heightened sensitivity to people and situations is an attribute you need for every dimension of networking. When talking to networking partners, potential partners, and people they refer you to, it helps to be able to "read between the lines." That's not to say that people aren't being candid with you. Rather, it's about being able to hear the subtext in a conversation, to pick up something in the other person's tone of voice or body language that indicates a need or preference that hasn't been stated—and that you can respond to. Networkers want to see this sort of savvy in their partners and to feel confident that if they refer you to someone, you'll have a sense of awareness that reflects well on them.

You also need to be perceptive when it comes to recognizing opportunities. Good leads and potential networking partners often come from very unlikely sources and situations and they won't be spelled out as such. So you have to keep your eyes and ears open to uncover an opportunity that might be lying beneath the surface—and then, of course, follow up on it.

Myth: Successful networkers are aggressive and pushy.

Fact: Successful networking has nothing to do with personality type.

Who you are certainly will affect how you approach the networking process and the type and pace of activities you decide to undertake. But whether you're a shrinking violet or bold as brass, you can develop particular qualities that will make you a good networker. How you use these qualities in a way that makes you comfortable then becomes a matter of personal style. (I'll give you some tips on how to do that in the section on "Developing Your Own Style.")

Yes, it's true that *some* successful networkers may by nature be more aggressive than others. But don't assume that it's their hard-driving style that makes networking work for them. (In fact, sometimes the exact opposite can happen—pushing too hard can turn off the very people you want to reach.) Successful networking is more directly related to personal commitment, good organization, sustained effort, and good follow-through than it is to any particular personality trait.

Good Listener

If you're a good listener, you're truly paying attention to what the other person is saying and not just waiting for him or her to finish so that you can talk. And when you're speaking with a networking partner—or someone you'd like to have as one—you *want* to listen. That's how you discover common ground on which to build your relationship. That's how you find out about the other person's interests, needs, and desires so that you know how to help them out in the future. Get the conversational ball rolling by asking questions that people enjoy answering—everyone likes to discuss things that interest them. And make sure to ask questions that you really want to hear the answers to. The ideal is to have a conversation that does both.

In case you're saying to yourself, "No problem, I'm a great listener," consider this cautionary tale. Over 800 men and women of different professions, ages, and management levels were asked whether their predominant conversational style was to listen or to talk. Some 90 percent believed they were primarily good listeners. But, when they were tested, they found out that they were usually talkers.

Trusting and Trustworthy

Trust is one of the most important elements in any relationship so don't forget it when it comes to your networking partners. You have to trust that your partners are responsible and will follow through as they've promised in a way that's appropriate to the circumstances. Since your partners have to be able to assume that your word is as good as gold, make sure you only promise what you can—and will—deliver. And a networking partner referring you to others has to feel secure that you not only know how to handle yourself appropriately in any situation but will also make them look good.

Goal-Oriented

Networking can seem like a very haphazard process unless you're clearly focused on what you want to get out of it and how you plan to get there. Good networkers identify a goal they want to achieve and set a time frame in which to accomplish it—for example, signing on three new clients in the next six months or speaking at an industry conference within the next two years. Then you can create a specific and realistic action plan outlining the steps you need to take to reach that goal, including the help you'll need from each of your networking partners.

Myth: People who practice networking are usually manipulative.

Fact: Manipulators, who are concerned only with their own self-interest, can't thrive in a networking environment oriented toward mutual benefit and sustaining relationships.

In a healthy networking relationship, neither person seeks to have power over the other; instead, each uses his or her power to help the other. Controlling a situation so that it works to your advantage may be acceptable for a while, but once a networking partner begins to feel used, he or she will bring the relationship to a quick end. Manipulators may indeed achieve short-term gains, but they ruin their chances of reaping long-term benefits.

There's a big difference, however, between manipulating someone and providing good direction. Making specific, realistic requests of your networking partners—and being willing to respond to theirs—isn't taking advantage of them; it's simply making it easier for them to provide the help you need.

Strategic Thinking

Strategic thinkers are always evaluating options and opportunities to figure out the most productive way to get the best results for themselves and their networking partners. They look at how they can achieve mutual benefit from each networking action and interaction, taking those steps that will both further their cause and meet the needs of the other person. They are constantly evaluating priorities, assessing the possible impact of their actions, and making the most efficient use of their resources to make sure that they get the optimal results.

Myth: Networkers are "takers," not "givers."

Fact: Networkers are takers *and* givers.

I've said it before and I'll say it again: the whole point of the networking process is *mutual* benefit. When you enter into a networking association, the good faith understanding is that you'll be considering ways to help your networking partner while he or she is doing the same for you. If you owe someone, you've got to find ways to give back. Upset the balance of reciprocity by too much taking and not enough giving and you'll quickly be persona non grata among your former networking partners.

Focused yet Flexible

Good networkers realize that the best-laid plans can often go astray. Circumstances change and people who promise to help can get sidetracked by their own professional or personal concerns. Think of your networking plan as a roadmap to success: there are usually any number of avenues that will lead you to your destination. If you unexpectedly find a path blocked for you, detour to an alternate route.

THE ACTIONS OF A GOOD NETWORKER

Cultivating these positive qualities is one part of the equation that adds up to being a good networker, but it's not the whole sum. You also have to *do* something with these qualities and translate attitudes into actions.

Be Prepared

A good networker is like a good scout—always prepared. Successful networkers do their homework before every networking

The Actions of a Good Networker
Be prepared Be specific Follow through Keep working at it

encounter. They think about what they want to accomplish and get the information they need to make it a productive meeting that focuses on mutual benefit. The more you know about the interests and needs of your networking partners, the better you can determine how they can help you and what you can do for them. And making that kind of extra effort lets your partner know that you're a thoughtful and serious networker who is worth developing a relationship with.

Be Specific

Successful networkers are the ones who don't expect their partners to be mind-readers or to do their thinking for them. A good networker would cringe at the thought of saying, "What can you do for me?" Rather, he or she approaches the other person with a clear, realistic request for assistance, something like, "I know you're on an industrywide task force with the public relations director at XYZ Company and I'd like to get in touch with her about promoting her CEO as an industry spokesperson. The industry really needs unified leadership and I think XYZ could provide it. Could you set up a conference call to introduce me to her so that I could follow up with a get-acquainted lunch?"

Follow Through

In networking, following through is critical. Do what you say you're going to do for your networking partners—and if you can't or won't, then don't promise. Follow up on the leads and suggestions they give you and report back to them on your progress. Look at it this way: you expect your networking partners to come through with what they promised and they have a right to expect the same of you.

Keep Working At It

Successful people work at networking. The level of effort you put into it is directly related to what you'll get out of it. Being a passive networker simply won't work. To get the results you want, your motto has to be: "Try, try again."

So now you have the basic equation for successful networking: Qualities + Actions = Results. With this solid foundation, you can start to formulate a networking mindset and process that will serve you well for the rest of your life.

DOS AND DON'TS

Do: Make specific commitments to yourself and your networking partners.

Do: Be clear and focused about your networking goals and
strategies.

Do: Work on building relationships that will last a lifetime.

Do: Be on the lookout for ways to help your networking
partners.

Do: Be creative and resourceful in your approach to networking.

Don't: Be a passive networker.

Don't: Expect your networking partners to do your thinking
for you.

Don't: Be a "taker" or a manipulator.

MAKING
CONNECTIONS:
WHO AND HOW

Picture yourself in situations like these:

Doug, a paralegal with a law firm, is mingling at the company's holiday party when he sees Miriam, a partner in the firm, who has been working on some high-visibility cases that really interest Doug. He'd love to get on a project team with her. Is there anything he can do in this situation to further his cause?

Danielle is a senior sales representative for a printing company. She wants to find companies that would be interested in customizing brochures by using pre-printed paper stock that can be laser-printed with personalized sales messages. She calls Susan, a client services manager for a telecommunications company, and invites her to lunch to pick her brain about possible prospects. What can Danielle do to make it worth Susan's time and effort to help?

Barbara, an accounting firm tax partner, runs into Ned, who is an account executive for an advertising agency. One of his clients is a privately held company that makes residential and commercial windows and doors. Barbara has some interesting tax ideas for own-

ers wanting to get more cash out of their private businesses. How should she approach Ned about making a connection with his client?

While the details in these scenarios obviously won't reflect your particular experience, the idea of recognizing a possible opportunity but not knowing how to act on it is familiar to all of us. Just how do you go about getting the networking ball rolling? If you follow the practical suggestions in this chapter, you'll never be caught short again. (By the way, to find out the next networking steps in each of the scenarios above, turn to the end of the chapter.)

Questions to Get You Started
What do I want to accomplish? Who can help me accomplish my goal? How do I go about cultivating these people?

WHAT DO I WANT TO ACCOMPLISH?

Most successful people have gotten where they are because they set specific goals for themselves to work toward. It makes perfect sense—if you don't have a vision of where you want to be, how will you know when you're there? So the first step in successful networking is clearly defining your networking goals, both short- and long-term. If you're looking for a new job, what kind of industry, company, and position do you want to work in? If you have your own business and are looking to expand it, how many and what kind of new clients do you want to recruit? How much income do you want to generate over what period of time?

If you work within an organization, is your goal to earn a promotion or to move to a different department? Do you want to use networking within the company to build support for key concepts and plans? to encourage group problem-solving? to foster better interdepartmental communications? to focus attention on pivotal business issues? to boost morale? to create team spirit? Are you looking to network outside your company to bring in new business? to gain industry expertise? to develop recognition as an industry expert? to share technical or scientific information with other specialists working on similar projects? to plan your next career move?

In your personal life, are you interested in gaining political advantage by running for office, being named to a political appointment, or influencing policy issues? Do you want to develop a power base in your community by taking a leadership role in local organizations and events? Are you interested in social standing, such as membership in the right clubs or invitations to certain high-profile events?

WHO CAN HELP ME ACCOMPLISH MY GOAL?

With your goal set, you can begin the process of identifying the networking partners who are most likely to help you achieve it. (If you're pursuing goals in different areas of your life at the same time, you'll probably have different sets of people.) First, go through your Rolodex and consider everyone you know—coworkers, friends, family members, fellow alumni, people in your apartment building, neighborhood, or community. Sociologists point out that each of us knows 200 or more people who pass though our lives with some frequency, so you've got a pretty big pool to start with. Be creative in assessing how each of these people might be able to help you, either because of what they do or who they know. Obviously, businesspeople who work in the industry you are in, or want to be in, are the first choices for professional networking partners. But some well-connected people who may not seem to be natural allies in helping you reach an immediate goal are well worth cultivating because they might be able to help you attain other objectives down the line.

Where to Meet Business Networking Partners

At work
Industry conferences, seminars, and lectures
Alumni events
Meetings of professional organizations
Electronic bulletin boards

You should also consider expanding your scope far beyond the people you already know to encompass the many others out there who are potential networking partners for you. When it comes to meeting other professionals, keep your antennae tuned at industry conferences, seminars, and lectures; at alumni events; at meetings of professional organizations; and at work, where you want to look for opportunities to cultivate people in other departments and divisions. Good places to develop networking connections in your personal life (which, by the way, can also carry over into your professional activities) include your church or temple, the gym, continuing education classes, sports events, political functions, and gatherings sponsored by charitable groups or neighborhood associations.

Late-twentieth-century technology is also introducing a whole new way of expanding networking possibilities—electronic bulletin boards. With a personal computer and a modem, the world can become your networking universe. Some 12 million Americans are already taking a ride on the information highway, linked to commercial online companies like CompuServe, America On-line, and Prodigy or tapped into Internet, the worldwide web of computer networks.

More and more networking and career-related bulletin boards are popping up on various computer-based services. You can participate

---

Finding Personal Networking Partners

Church, temple, or other religious organizations
Sports and fitness activities
Charitable organizations or social causes
Continuing education classes
Social clubs
Cultural events
Political organizations and campaigns
Alumni groups
Neighborhood associations
PTA and other school groups
Electronic bulletin boards

---

in networking groups, contact other professionals in your field, peruse employment listings, and join in discussions of career issues. And electronically conversing with like-minded people through bulletin boards dedicated to specific topics and interests might help you find personal networking partners as well. I know of someone who has made both personal and professional connections in cyberspace. Angela is a graphic designer in Boston who participates in a number of Internet forums. She regularly communicates with Hal in San Diego, who not only shares her interest in Native American issues and culture but also put her in touch with a friend of his in Hawaii who was looking for a designer to work with on a project.

Some experts think that on-line networking will become the wave of the future. I'm not so sure. Networking as we've been exploring it is a highly personal interaction that requires constant nurturing to yield mutual benefit. I'm not convinced that this can be achieved through matching hopes, dreams, and styles with electronic pen pals. But if you do decide to venture into cyberspace networking,

I believe you'll be most successful over the long term if you follow up electronic matchmaking with more personal contact with your partners to maintain an active interest in each other's welfare.

HOW DO I GO ABOUT CULTIVATING THESE PEOPLE?

So far, so good. You've figured out your networking goal and targeted some people you think would be good partners to help you achieve it. But now comes the part that makes a lot of people quake in their boots. What exactly do you do? What do you say? What's appropriate and what's being pushy? Many of us aren't comfortable meeting strangers or making small talk. Many of us have a hard time asking for favors. And many of us hate to "owe" anything to anyone.

First of all, it helps to remember our definition of networking: the consistent application of interpersonal skills in cultivating individuals for mutual benefit and lasting relationships. Sure, some people are more socially adept than others. But *all* of us have interpersonal skills that can be developed, refined, and enhanced the more we use them. And it's a lot easier to ask for help if it's understood up front that you'll return the courtesy at some later date because this is a long-term relationship that depends on each person coming through for the other. Hopefully, looking at networking from this perspective will help you get beyond any discomfort or fear you have about the process and allow you to get on with doing it. So let's get started.

LEARN ALL YOU CAN ABOUT YOUR NETWORKING PARTNERS

A big part of successful networking is relationship-building with your partners. And that requires two-way communication in which you listen as much as—or perhaps even more than—you talk. Talking more than we listen is an easy habit to fall into, especially if we enjoy what we do, feel sure of our skills and expertise, and have

Connecting in Cyberspace

With some 33,000 bulletin boards nationwide, the trick to technological networking is to target your efforts.

- *Identify a bulletin board that attracts businesspeople.* Since the whole electronic bulletin board concept is rather new, companies may not yet have subscriber profiles. If they do, pick one that matches your needs. If no information is available, tell the company what you want to do and see if they will allow you to put out a request for information.
- *Post your bulletin board request.* Consider your potential networking partner's needs first, then follow with your own. Be specific about what you want and what you have to give in developing a networking relationship. Try something like this:

Networkers: Let's Swap

Well-respected purchasing manager seeks networking partners who want more contacts among suppliers of hardware machinery equipment serving East Coast hardware manufacturers. I need: Contacts among West Coast hardware manufacturers.

- *Screen responses.* You're apt to get a lot of undesirable responses simply because of the sheer number of people noting your request. Following up on promising responses to discover if there's a real fit shouldn't be hard, but it can be time-consuming. Keep your communications confined to the network until you're satisfied that you have a serious, qualified potential partner. Then consider a phone conference or, if possible, a meeting.
- *Exchange expectations.* Here's where the relationship-building starts, and all the steps that apply to networking as defined in this book apply to on-line situations as well.

a healthy sense of self-esteem. It's natural and comfortable to talk about things that interest us and so we tend to guide the conversation to areas where we're familiar with the subject matter. The bottom line is that we often talk, talk, talk. But that defeats the purpose of networking. The object of a networking conversation is to *share* information and learn as much about the other person as you want him or her to know about you.

Cultivating Your Networking Partners

Learn all you can about your networking partners.
Satisfy your networking partners' needs first.
Keep the business part of networking conversations short and simple.
Always let your networking partners know you're thinking about them.

I think many of us tend to talk a lot not because we don't care about the other person, but because we simply don't know how to draw him or her out. Well, here, in a nutshell, is the simplest and most effective way to get another person to talk: ask questions. In networking situations, you want to focus your questions to get useful information about the other person's expertise, opinions, goals, priorities, likes, and dislikes so that you can figure out how your abilities, objectives, and strategies match up with what they need and value. You should get a good sense of their strengths and weaknesses in order to know what areas they'll best be able to offer you assistance with. And you should also get an idea of what they need so that you can be on the lookout for opportunities for them.

Asking questions, however, doesn't mean giving the other person the third degree. It's meant to be a conversational device that allows for a give-and-take of information, a way to introduce topics to keep the talk flowing. And it's easy to weave pointed questions into a general discussion. If you mention a movie you saw last weekend, for example, you've got a natural opening to talk about your hobbies and interests and to find out what the other person likes to do in his or her spare time.

Here are some different kinds of topics to explore with your networking partners:

PROFESSIONAL

- Most satisfying job-related projects
- Greatest professional strengths
- Any areas of expertise recognized by the person's company, industry, or professional peers
- Whether the person represents his or her company or industry at industry gatherings
- Whether he or she speaks to groups, roundtables, or public or government forums on company or industry issues

PERSONAL

- Family background
- Sports, hobbies, and leisure activities
- Membership or leadership roles in social clubs, community organizations, and so forth
- Preferred social activities
- Participation in community, neighborhood, and cultural events

NETWORKING

- Frequency and methods
- Personal goals
- Kinds of activities that have paid off and that haven't worked
- What's satisfying and unsatisfying about networking

- Types of networking referrals he or she values
- Follow-up techniques with valued referrals
- Long- and short-term payoff
- Most memorable networking experiences
- Networking situations better forgotten
- Types of people he or she is currently networking with
- Styles most and least complementary to personal goals

By delving into these kinds of topics with each of your networking partners over a period of time, you'll acquire a rich and detailed portrait of these people—their goals, motivations, preferences, and needs—that will guide you as you find ways to work effectively together.

SATISFY YOUR NETWORKING PARTNERS' NEEDS FIRST

Making the first move by doing something for your networking partners before they do anything for you can be a smart strategy. You're more likely to get their attention and maintain their interest. And there's a good chance that they'll then feel more obligated to return the favor by looking out for opportunities that would benefit you. Being the first to act also implies that you're networking vigorously right from the beginning of a relationship. When you're open to seeing the opportunities that are all around you, you'll be able to identify the ones that will help your networking partners.

Essentially, you want to gain a reputation as being someone who is good to network with. As a result, over time you will attract better and better networking partners; and the synergy of networking activity, as well as the benefits you derive from it, will accelerate to higher and higher levels. As you and your networking partners get swept up in the energy of effective networking, everyone experiences gratifying results that justify their involvement.

KEEP THE BUSINESS PART OF NETWORKING CONVERSATIONS SHORT AND SIMPLE

French philosopher and mathematician Blaise Pascal once apologized for writing a friend a long letter, explaining that he didn't have time to write a short one. Being brief and to the point doesn't always come naturally to people and it takes significant practice to learn how to do it. But it's a skill that's important to have in the networking arena.

In your networking encounters, you don't want to spend the entire time together talking about business. Rather, you want to quickly and efficiently address networking matters so that you can take time to enjoy each other's company in the kind of casual and friendly give-and-take that cements any relationship. At a business lunch, for example, seasoned networkers may take the first 15 minutes to trade networking information about what has happened since their last meeting and agree on next steps, then devote the rest of the time to talking about other areas of interest, such as industry news, world affairs, sports, community events, and so forth.

To help you get the hang of it, try using this outline to focus your networking conversations, whether they're face-to-face or over the phone:

    I. Review the steps you agreed to take after the last meeting.
    II. Summarize your progress so far.
    III. Explain your next steps.
    IV. Tell your partner about any emerging opportunities that could benefit him or her.
    V. Have your networking partner respond in kind.

ALWAYS LET YOUR NETWORKING PARTNERS KNOW YOU'RE THINKING ABOUT THEM

With all the information you've collected about your networking partners, it's a cinch to be thoughtful and sensitive to things that might be of interest to them. I'm not talking here about being on the lookout for business opportunities, which is the very foundation of your networking relationship. I'm referring to the small kindnesses that go above and beyond the call of duty.

For instance, what about clipping an interesting article related to a partner's job and sending it with a brief note saying, "I thought you might enjoy this." Or making a call to let a partner know that his or her favorite band is playing in the area and you wanted to make sure he or she knew about it. Considerate gestures like these don't take much time or effort on your part but can be really appreciated by those on the receiving end. Most people don't go out of their way like this and it marks you as someone special. Relating what you read and hear about to your partners' personal, professional, and networking interests is a clear statement that you value your relationship with them and that your connection transcends the business sphere.

SOME SPECIAL ADVICE FOR PROFESSIONALS

Professionals—doctors, dentists, lawyers, accountants, and others needing special qualifications to practice—face special challenges when it comes to networking. Traditionally, professionals have felt most comfortable interacting with their peers and may not have aggressively reached out to network with those outside their profession. But networking harder among your colleagues isn't likely to keep you moving ahead in a highly competitive environment. If you want to be successful, you need to broaden the scope of your networking relationships beyond your friends in the profession.

The idea of broadening your contact base, however, might raise some critical issues for you related to standards and traditions in your field. What's considered appropriate in my profession? Are there any restrictions on how and with whom I can network?

Having worked extensively with professionals, I've come to believe that some of the difficulties they have in networking with the lay community stem from the days before the 1978 Supreme Court decision allowing professionals to advertise and promote themselves just like any other businesspeople. Before that, ethics committees in most fields didn't allow practitioners to solicit clients directly. To get prospective clients to contact them, many professionals became quite adept at networking with fellow doctors, lawyers, or accountants. But they had little experience making connections with laypeople.

Many young professionals who began practicing after the Supreme Court ruling don't have as much of a problem with questions of propriety. And older practitioners who still have lingering doubts are having to reorient themselves to today's realities. The bottom line is that you're free to promote yourself in any way you choose. And what's "professional" is up to your discretion.

If you feel uncomfortable interacting with the general public, you need to stretch your "comfort zone" when it comes to the activities you undertake to make connections outside of your profession. Simply put, if you want to grow your practice, you have to find ways to reach out to the larger community.

Some think that advertising is the answer. I don't. It's true that advertising builds awareness. But in the media clutter of contemporary society, where people are bombarded with advertising messages from all directions, it takes a lot of money and a long-term effort to develop the kind of awareness that brings business in the door. I believe that a determined professional with a simple yet sound networking plan can achieve results that are just as effective as those from advertising — and perhaps even more so. Let's take a look at some ways you can begin to expand your network.

- *Reevaluate the rule that says my work comes first.* Some professionals consistently avoid networking among laypeople by saying that they'll network when their work is done—which for a busy professional is never! Just as you find time to attend professional association or society meetings to network among your colleagues, you can find time for other networking activities as well. Simply put your mind to it and get started.

■ *Share insights about your profession.* If you find yourself at a loss about what to say to potential networking partners outside of your profession, consider explaining your professional views on a landmark case that's been in the news lately, a breakthrough scientific discovery, or impending legislation that will affect businesses. Focus on a subject that laypeople are hearing conflicting opinions, advice, and promises about, and share your "insider's" perspective. This allows you to display your professional expertise without appearing to blow your own horn. And because of your professional credentials, your interpretation of complex issues in your field is likely to be readily accepted by laypeople. There's a good chance that the people you're talking to will repeat your remarks to others, dropping your name along the way.

■ *Join organizations outside of your profession.* This is a great way to meet people outside your professional milieu while doing something you enjoy. Before committing yourself to a particular group, though, look over the membership roster to make sure that the people you'll be spending time with are decision-makers or have influence useful to your professional position. Also be careful about volunteering your professional services to an organization. If you're an accountant and you become the organization's treasurer, for example, your contribution could be taken for granted because that's your profession. Look at how your experience gives you special insights that could help the organization, then aim for a committee post in which you can apply those insights.

This can take many forms. If you're a law partner with a general practice firm and your nonprofessional organization is trying to establish and sponsor a youth camp, contribute your business sense and negotiating skills to make a good deal. If you're a physician with office staffing experience, help the reorganization committee develop staffing standards to make the group more effective and efficient. Exercising diverse skills can give you a great deal of satisfaction and you'll gain more visibility among the members for offering insights and contributions in areas they didn't expect.

- *Budget your time.* To avoid networking burnout, treat networking demands on your time in the same way you handle professional demands—not by working harder, but by working smarter. On the job, you practice a kind of professional triage to get demands on your time back into alignment. Using this technique in other areas of your life will help keep you appropriately involved in activities that interest you and enrich your life.
- *Learn from the lay community's approach to networking.* Now that you've gained a higher level of comfort in reaching out to the lay community, use the techniques described in this book to become as consummate a networker among others as you are among professionals. It's every bit as enjoyable as networking with your colleagues and your practice will reap the rewards for a long time to come.

MEANWHILE, BACK AT OUR OPENING SCENARIOS . . .

Remember the three networking scenarios at the beginning of this chapter? These are appropriate next steps for Doug, Danielle, and Barbara to take:

> Doug, the paralegal, doesn't approach his firm's partner Miriam about getting involved with her high-profile cases until he does his homework and has something to offer her in return. He searches through his address book to find college chums who are now working for companies that his firm would value as clients. He then approaches Miriam to express his interest in helping with her cases, mentioning that he has been thinking about ways to tap certain companies where he knows, through some of his friends from college, that there's a need for the firm's services.
>
> Danielle, the printing company sales representative, tells her networking partner Susan that she would welcome some sugges-

tions about the kinds of companies that would be hot prospects for her employer's preprinted paper. In return, Danielle offers to give Susan some free laser-ready paper to experiment with to see if it will work for Susan's company.

Barbara, the accounting firm partner, explains her tax ideas for private business owners to Ned, the advertising agency account executive, and asks if his window manufacturing client—and any other closely held companies that are clients of Ned's agency— might be interested. She then brainstorms with Ned to see how introducing her to his clients could help his image.

DOS AND DON'TS

Do: Be creative in assessing how different people might be good networking partners.

Do: Consider electronic networking via computer bulletin boards if you're comfortable with the technology.

Do: Ask your networking partners questions to learn all you can about them.

Do: Make the first move in a networking relationship by doing something for the other person before he or she does anything for you.

Do: Gain a reputation as someone who is good to network with.

Do: Mix business with pleasure in developing networking relationships.

Don't: Feel uncomfortable about asking your networking partners for help—it's understood that you'll be reciprocating.

Don't: Make your partners feel like you're giving them the third degree when you ask questions—questions should be part of conversational give-and-take.

Don't: Neglect cultivating well-connected individuals because they can't help you right now—they might be able to assist in the future.

Don't: Dominate the conversation in networking encounters.

Developing Your Own Style: Personality and Preferences

Which of these profiles describes your personality?

a) You tend to have a relaxed, go-with-the-flow attitude toward life. You adapt easily to any situation, like spontaneity and variety, and aren't very interested in discipline or detail. You usually live in the moment and are generally satisfied with your life.

b) You're interested in a wide range of things and are curious to find out as much as you can about them. You join groups and pursue activities because you like sharing ideas, information, and experiences. You enjoy connecting with others as well as making a contribution to whatever you participate in.

c) You're a thinker and planner. You tend to analyze situations, look at the risks and rewards, and anticipate probable outcomes. You're thoughtful and logical and good at orchestrating situations to bring about the results you want.

d) You're a mover and shaker with a strong personality who enjoys being in the spotlight. You're decisive, action-oriented, and bursting with energy. You tend to be a leader, getting others excited about your ideas and activities.

Of course, none of these profiles can capture the unique essence of your personality. And you may identify with elements of more than one. But they can be useful in helping you assess and develop the networking style that's most appropriate for you. Even though the principles of successful networking that I'm telling you about throughout this book remain constant, what varies from person to person is how these principles can be tailored to fit individual personalities and preferences. In other words, there's no one networking mold that everyone has to fit into. Rather, you need to figure out how to get things done in a way that you feel comfortable with. Otherwise, you simply won't do them. And then you're not networking.

Factors That Influence Your Networking Style
Your personality The type of work you do How much effort you put into networking

Several factors influence how you approach networking. Obviously, your personality and temperament play a big part. For instance, let's take two people on opposite ends of the personality spectrum. Josh tends to be quiet and reserved, and he hates to go to industry events by himself and talk to strangers. So he might start his networking ball rolling by asking for personal referrals from people he already knows. Kristin, on the other hand, would call the Queen of England without thinking twice if that's what she felt she had to do to achieve her goal. There are seemingly no limits to the approaches she would feel comfortable taking.

So if you find me suggesting a technique that you can't imagine yourself doing, don't do it—yet. There's always another route you can take. The point is, do *something* to get you started and keep you moving. Over time, you will need to think about stretching and pushing yourself a bit. And after a while, I hope you'll gain the confidence to try those networking moves you never thought you'd be able to do.

The type of work you do can also make a difference in your networking style. A lot of jobs involve frequent and often intense interaction with other people. Public relations practitioners, salespeople, service representatives, teachers, and health-care providers, for example, are constantly meeting new people who could be potential networking partners. They may not have the need or desire to attend a lot of events where they'd be chatting with yet more strangers; they might find a series of one-on-one encounters much more satisfying. Many individuals, though, don't have the chance to get out and about on their jobs—people who work in an accounting department, for example, or computer programmers—and their contacts may be limited to a few other people in their office. For these individuals, the idea of having a cross-section of people from all walks of life in the same room at the same time just waiting to be approached could be very appealing.

A third element is how much time and effort you put into networking. The type and frequency of activities you undertake are often determined by how much you want something, as well as how much time you can carve out of your busy schedule to give to networking. Sometimes when you have a lot of personal and professional irons in the fire, you'll choose to do no more than the minimum required to remind your networking partners that you're still alive. Other times when you really need something—a lead to a new job or client, for example—you'll be going at your networking like there's no tomorrow.

There are as many different styles of networking as there are individuals doing it. But I've noticed that people tend to fall into a few broad categories that relate to the four personality types described in the quiz at the beginning of this chapter.

Networking Styles
The Laid-Back Networker The Involved Networker The Strategic Networker The High-Energy Networker

THE LAID-BACK NETWORKER

The laid-back networker (Type A in the personality profile) is as easygoing about networking activities as he or she is about everything else in life. Laid-back types generally aren't all that rigorous about setting goals and making plans. If an opportunity presents itself, they'll respond. But they don't usually go out of their way to find networking partners and activities; they wait to be approached. And since they tend to be affable, accessible, and easy to talk to, people frequently do come to them. However, because their networking style is as open and unfocused as their personality, laid-back networkers often need prompting to make commitments and to follow through. This style can be effective, but it takes much longer for efforts to pay off since casual relationships that aren't carefully cultivated won't start to bear fruit for quite some time.

If you have this style, making time for networking is relatively easy. You don't have to plan for anything particular to happen. But you do need to be able to recognize opportunity when it knocks. For example, if you're asked to be part of an interesting special project team being formed in your company, then go for it—even if it means putting in extra hours. If you meet an interesting businessperson outside your company, be responsive to this chance meeting. Show interest in his or her activities. Ask thoughtful questions that demonstrate your concern for things that are important to the other person. You never know when this relationship will come in handy. Your contact could provide a reality check for your ideas, some wisdom that is counter to conventional industry beliefs, or even a pathway to a job opportunity at some future time.

Also, don't overlook your neighbors as potential networking partners. Without venturing very far from your own front door, you can find ways to apply your business skills to social and community situations. For example, many communities have block associations that organize everything from spring curbside clean-ups to neighborhood parties. Laid-back networkers can also be found working with community organizations like the Little League, Boys and Girls Clubs, or the Police Athletic League, that focus on helping youngsters. The networking in these situations tends to be very casual and arises naturally, over time, out of shared interests and goals.

Another long-term approach for the laid-back networker is participating in self-improvement programs. Businesspeople of this type often take evening adult education classes at local colleges because they can learn a lot in a concentrated time period. You might also think of trying a group like Toastmasters International (see Appendix for a geographic listing of Toastmasters around the country), which helps people develop their public speaking skills. This kind of activity yields a double benefit: enhancing your ability to communicate effectively—a valued skill in the business world—as well as effortlessly broadening your base of contacts.

Laid-back networking appeals to many people because it doesn't require a major commitment or a huge effort. It's simply adding another layer of awareness to activities you already take part in. Yet even this relaxed approach can yield good networking results and lay a foundation for future interaction should you ever decide you want to step up the pace.

THE INVOLVED NETWORKER

The involved networker (Type B) is a joiner who likes being with people and sharing his or her many interests with others. Involved networkers tend to be engaged in a broad variety of activities that may or may not have immediate networking potential. They'll take some risks in developing relationships and find value in making the contact regardless of the outcome. These people recognize and take advantage of networking possibilities that cross their paths but aren't particularly aggressive in ferreting out or creating opportunities. If this is your style, you want to be more proactive in identifying and boldly following through on the different networking options you're coming across in the course of your activities.

If you're an involved networker and you're asked to be on a special project team at work, your motives for joining the group would be to find out more about how the firm works, to meet peers and managers from different areas, and to make a contribution to the team and the company. If you meet an interesting businessperson outside your company, your inquisitive nature can serve you well. Ask questions to find common ground that can serve as the basis for a continuing relationship. Also learn about each other's capabilities and areas of expertise in case an opportunity arises for one of you to refer the other. Keep the relationship moving along and continue to have regular conversations where a good information exchange takes place.

Use this same approach in having useful conversations with colleagues in your organization. Concentrate on seeking out individuals who not only complement your interests but who also can increase awareness of your skills and abilities. Remember, people talk. If you project a positive image as someone who is skilled, experienced, and concerned about others, you may find unsolicited offers and overtures coming your way.

Since you tend to be a joiner by nature, make sure to take part in industry associations that will help you broaden your connections and visibility outside of your company. In your personal life, make it a point not only to network more consciously in the organizations you already belong to but also to join other groups that will both suit your interests and provide good networking possibilities. Religious, charitable, and cultural organizations are only a few of the types of groups that often need people with business skills to help them with a variety of tasks and problems. Getting involved is not only fun and rewarding, as you already know, but it can also put you in close contact with influential people you would not ordinarily meet.

The Four Networking Styles

	Laid-Back	Involved	Strategic	High-Energy
Style	Passive	Responsive	Focused	Assertive
Level of Effort/ Commitment	Low	Moderate	High	High
Approach	Casual	Low-Key	Planned	Dynamic
Goal	Awareness	Participation	Achievement	Leadership
Partners	Peers	Peers and Managers	Peers and Managers	Movers and Shakers

THE STRATEGIC NETWORKER

The strategic networker (Type C) usually doesn't do anything without having a well-developed plan. These strategists go about working their plans with quiet dedication, keeping their cards close to the vest. They only expose that part of their strategy that is necessary to get to the next step. When seen in its entirety, however, the strategic networker's plan is admired for its careful construction and smooth implementation. Strategic networkers know exactly what they want and, with focused energy and absolute determination, they make it happen.

Strategic networkers are results-oriented and usually make good use of their own and other people's time. And since it's in their nature to anticipate consequences and see next steps, they're able—and willing—to use their knowledge to help others. These qualities make them especially valuable networking partners.

If asked to be part of a companywide team effort, the strategic networker would get involved only to the extent that it served a master plan. He or she would think through the possible consequences of participation and figure out how it could serve as a stepping-stone to achieve an intermediate and/or long-term goal. If it serves their purpose, strategic networkers will take on leadership roles, but they don't ordinarily seek high visibility. Meeting an interesting businessperson outside of the company, the strategic networker would assess the possible mutual benefits of the relationship in light of how the other person fits into his or her plans.

If you're a strategic networker, you're probably doing pretty well for yourself. The one piece of advice I'd offer is to loosen up a bit and make room for serendipity. It's possible to be so wed to a particular strategy that you're not open to chance networking events and encounters that could yield benefits now or in the future.

THE HIGH-ENERGY NETWORKER

The high-energy networker (Type D) takes it to the limit. These dynamic people tend to have forceful personalities and ambitious goals and want to achieve leadership positions with high visibility.

The high-energy networker who is asked to participate in a company project team would seek a leadership role. He or she sees team involvement as part of a broader plan to become more visible in the company and uses team leadership as a means to even more important assignments—both within the company and, if the team is part of an industrywide effort, outside as well.

This kind of networking is highly active and focused. Like the strategic networker, the high-energy person's contact with others inside and outside the business is part of a carefully thought-out plan, based on questions like these: What kinds of contacts can help me broaden my awareness and insight into the activities of other divisions, other companies, the industry at large, and federal, state, and local issues and priorities? Which industry movers and shakers should I align with to further my value to my firm, my industry, other industries, and potential employers?

The networking mission of the high-energy person is to create a synergistic web of associations where he or she can cross-refer friends and acquaintances to a variety of people and organizations so that everyone gains from the visibility, personal involvement, and group interaction. This is a way for high-energy people to influence isssues for personal, corporate, industry, and/or public gain. They can also use their networking skills to lobby for change within their company to enhance their job responsibilities or position, to create awareness of their talents inside and outside the company environment, and to leapfrog into different but related industries.

High-energy networkers are usually just as active in developing good networking connections in their personal lives. As in business, they tend to be thinkers and doers who take a leadership role in the organizations they belong to. Their key issue, even in leisure activities, is how their participation supports their long-range objectives. Of course, it's admirable to altruistically serve the community with no ulterior motive but—as the high-energy networker would say—why not get more out of the experience by using your valuable time to help yourself at the same time you're helping others?

Take Louis, a marketing manager with a drug company. His business goal is to broaden his influence in the industry; so, as a complementary personal goal, he chooses participation in a health-care-related community project. This gives him the chance to apply his knowledge and skills to a good cause, while simultaneously interacting with a new but related group of people and gaining increased visibility within the community.

High-energy networkers also tend to take on responsibilities that will thrust them into the social spotlight where they can interact with the movers and shakers in the community. And they often find themselves in the thick of public policy issues, whether it's shaping educational programs through the local school board or leading a regional environmental initiative.

If you're a high-energy networker, there's one predicament you have to be careful to guard against: getting to the point at which displaying energy and enthusiasm is perceived by others as being overbearing, intimidating, or manipulative. Because you tend to have powerful personalities and the energy level of a hurricane, people who don't share these qualities can feel overwhelmed—if not bullied—when dealing with you. Successful networking depends on a spirit of cooperation, not coercion. So no matter how important or worthy your goal, be careful not to push so hard that others begin to resent what they view as a demanding style. Nobody likes to feel as if he or she has been run over by a Sherman Tank!

Now that you have some basic models of different networking styles, you can start to fashion the one that's right for you. Be realistic about the level of energy and commitment you're willing and able to put into networking right now, and act accordingly. You can always adjust your plan later as your interests and goals change. But no matter what, how, or how much you decide to do, start networking *now*.

DOS AND DON'TS

Do: Develop a networking style that complements your personality, type of work, and level of commitment.

Do: Integrate useful elements of other networking styles into your own.

Do: Be flexible in adjusting your style as your goals and needs change.

Don't: Think that there's one networking mold that everyone has to fit into.

Don't: Try to be someone you're not when it comes to networking—do what's comfortable for you.

Don't: Try too hard or do too little—find a comfortable balance.

THE SEVEN PRINCIPLES OF SUCCESSFUL NETWORKING

PRINCIPLE #1:
HAVE FUN

Who says networking has to be all work and no play? Not me. In fact, I believe having fun is the cornerstone of networking success. That's why I've listed it first. When I say fun, I'm not thinking of escape-from-reality kind of fun, but rather the kind of fun that generates mutual enthusiasm and synergy around something you believe in. Good networking depends on developing and maintaining a certain synergy with the people you interact with. And synergy comes from a common understanding of, and belief in, the objective of networking, plus enthusiasm for the results. Enthusiasm is the key because it can be so contagious.

Beginning networkers often make the mistake of thinking that networking encounters have to be serious, formal, outcome-oriented business meetings that involve a superior-subordinate relationship (with the person asking for help in the subordinate role). A lot of people also tend to see networking as a process that has to conform to certain procedural rules. If any of this were true, I probably wouldn't be networking myself—it certainly doesn't make networking seem very appealing.

The reality is that warm, thoughtful, and considerate networking is definitely O.K. In fact, relaxed interactions are likely to yield better, more satisfying outcomes than businesslike approaches. If more people saw networking as another form of friendly interaction instead of as a chore, I think everyone would be doing it and having a great time helping each other to be more effective.

Part of the pleasure of networking comes from simply having a good conversation with someone you enjoy being with. Along with any tangible benefits you may reap down the line from your networking encounters, you get the immediate satisfaction of connecting with another person.

So when you make a follow-up call to a networking partner, for instance, don't think it has to be a flat, formal, one-minute exchange focused only on what networking-related steps each of you has taken since the last time you touched base. Assuming that you can both take a few minutes out of your busy day just to chat, use the time to catch up on what's been happening on the job, exchange industry news, discuss last week's baseball game or a movie you've seen—in other words, talk about anything you have in common that will help strengthen the ties between you. Then your discussion of networking activities becomes an easy and natural extension of your broader relationship.

One of the best ways to make networking fun is to plan networking activities around social events. Depending on your different partners' tastes and preferences and the depth of your relationship, you can invite them to a sports or cultural event, suggest going to a community or neighborhood gathering, or entertain them at your home. In these situations, it's appropriate to include "significant others" if you think it will add to the comfort level and enjoyment of the activity. But don't forget that your purpose in being together is based on your networking relationship. So at some point make sure that you take a few minutes to have the kind of short, simple, focused conversation about networking matters that I outlined in the chapter on "Making Connections."

DOS AND DON'TS

Do: Be relaxed and friendly with your networking partners.

Do: Make your networking activities a natural extension of your broader relationship with a partner.

Do: Plan networking activities around social events.

Don't: Think of networking as a chore, but as a pleasure.

Don't: Be stiff and serious at meetings with your partners.

Don't: Make every networking call a formal business conversation.

PRINCIPLE #2: MAKE TIME AND USE IT WISELY

"I'd love to try networking, but I just don't have time."

Let's face it. If you wait until you have time to network, chances are you'll never do it. You have a demanding job or business. You have commitments to family and friends. You have personal interests and concerns you want to attend to. So when, you might ask, are you supposed to have the time to network?

The answer is that making time for networking is really an emotional commitment, not a lockstep schedule of hours and minutes necessary to keep the process moving. And the process advances differently for different people based on the goals they set for themselves and the commitment they make to reaching those goals. But no matter what level of effort you choose to put into it, you have to make networking an integral part of your life, not an occasional addition to it.

As the diagram below illustrates, people typically think of networking and the performance of their jobs as separate activities. That is, your job comes first, and if you ever have any spare time, you also network. The problem is, when pressed for time (and who isn't?), most of us tend to make our job or important personal activity the priority, and networking gets lost in the shuffle. And when you get caught up in your work, you might not even recognize a networking opportunity if it were offered to you on a silver platter. Conversely, if you single-mindedly pursue networking, you may not put enough energy into doing your job well. Both extremes are likely to produce negative results.

Your Job and Networking Should Complement Each Other

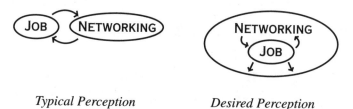

Typical Perception   *Desired Perception*

However, when you consider networking to be a useful complement to your job, you'll constantly migrate back and forth between the two. Viewed from this perspective, you're always looking for networking opportunities because you can see useful synergy between your job and your networking activity.

When you think about it, don't you usually find time do all the things that are important to you? My guess is that you can and do. Finding time for networking, then, should be given the same priority as anything else that you value. I know it's not always easy to juggle all these different activities. So here are some suggestions on how you can make better use of your time to accomplish everything you want to do.

DON'T OVERCOMMIT

A frequent trap we all fall into at times is making commitments to do more than we realistically can handle. It happens with networking, too. In the first rush of enthusiasm, you might find yourself making promises that you can't possibly keep if you still expect to do your job effectively and tend to all your personal responsibilities. So

---

Managing Your Time—and Yourself

Don't overcommit
Don't procrastinate
Don't use up your personal time
Set priorities
Be patient

---

be realistic. For example, if you really push yourself hard, you might be able to follow up on 10 networking contacts per week. But you can only do 5 comfortably. So set your goal for the 5. Making 5 successful contacts is far better for your psyche and continued networking enthusiasm than sacrificing another priority to achieve an arbitrary goal of 10.

If you set unrealistic or unreachable networking objectives for yourself and don't achieve them, you may be tempted to blame the process rather than admit that your goals were too high. And then you may come to the mistaken conclusion that networking just takes too much time. So don't sabotage yourself before you begin. Take the time up front—before you make any commitments to yourself and others—to decide what, given your personality and style, you can and will do effectively and well within a certain time frame.

At this point, nobody knows what your plan is, so there's no embarrassment if you decide to take it easy because you have a lot of other irons in the fire. Later, when you've made commitments to yourself and others, you can suffer from a bad reputation if you don't follow through. Remember, good networkers network. If you fail to deliver when someone is depending on you, the word will get around.

DON'T PROCRASTINATE

We've all had days at work when the most we've been able to accomplish is to push papers from one side of the desk to another. Impromptu meetings are called, colleagues come in with urgent requests, the phone never stops ringing. There will always be interruptions and unforeseen circumstances that keep us from doing the tasks we had planned. But not all day, every day. If you find that Scarlett O'Hara's famous line, "I'll think about it tomorrow," has become your motto, you need to examine how procrastination is playing a part in impairing your effectiveness.

Good networkers can usually avoid this by planning their networking work, then working their plan. You may think that this sounds simplistic and doesn't take into account mitigating circumstances. You're right. But if you don't think this way, it's much too easy to rationalize why you can't finish things. Have you heard the old saying, "If you need something done, ask a busy person to do it"? These individuals always seem to be able to take on extra responsibility, get the task done on time, and perform well enough that everyone is pleased with the result and their personal effectiveness. How do they always seem to have more time to do things than the rest of us?

I found some answers to this question in the best-selling book *The Seven Habits of Highly Effective People*, in which author Stephen R. Covey profiles a number of high-achievement people and traces the reasons for their success. There are several common threads among the factors credited for the success of these very busy, involved, and committed people. They all have good organizational skills, a narrow but integrated focus, and an "effectiveness" orientation. In choosing activities that would further their careers or help them reach professional, political, social, or personal goals, they only accept responsibility for priorities they deeply believe in. They exercise discretion and have the ability to say no to important and worthwhile causes that don't fit their priorities.

So take a cue from these busy, high-performance individuals. Be focused, be decisive, don't put things off, and get your networking job done thoroughly and well.

DON'T USE UP YOUR PERSONAL TIME

People who think of networking as a totally separate activity from their job have to make time to do it after working hours. But if your whole life consists of "job work" all day and "networking work" on nights and weekends, you're going to end up with a classic case of networking burnout. Everyone needs personal time and space to relax and recharge. Letting your networking time regularly infringe on your private time can make you angry and resentful, and perhaps even tempt you to give up on networking altogether because it's just too much trouble.

To avoid this problem, successful networkers do most of their networking during or immediately after the work day. This way, you can easily reach the people you need to help you; and you reinforce the concept that networking is a productive, useful part of your job. I'm not suggesting that you let your work suffer in any way because of the time you devote to networking. But everyone can carve out a few minutes to make a couple of phone calls, perhaps by coming to the office a few minutes early or leaving a few minutes late. And it's easy to meet your networking partners for lunch, or for coffee, drinks, or dinner after work.

Sure, there will be some networking tasks you choose to do at home, just as you sometimes bring work home from the office to get a head start on a project or, more often, to simply catch up. But make sure that any networking tasks you take home are very focused one-time or short-term activities. If you keep dragging home a long networking "To Do" list that you never quite get around to addressing, you can begin to resent networking as a burden that never ends. While the process is indeed a long-term effort, the trick is to break it down into manageable tasks and do a few every day so that you feel a sense of progress and accomplishment.

SET PRIORITIES

Even if you set realistic networking goals for yourself, you can't get everything done at once. So you have to get your priorities straight, deciding what's most important and assigning an order to your tasks. After determining your priorities, consider how different tasks relate to each other. If you've chosen carefully, they should connect into a web of interrelated activities to help you reach your goal with reasonable effort. Be systematic. And remember to pace yourself. Just take one step at a time and feel a sense of accomplishment for each task you complete.

BE PATIENT

Well-coordinated networking with high payoff potential takes time because it's a process of making good connections, not just good contacts. It's much like the natural process of developing friends versus simply having a number of acquaintances. Because you've experienced many friendships over your lifetime, you understand that this is a slow process of mutual exploration, testing, and confirmation of your relationships. You understand that it takes time so you're patient as you allow friendships to unfold naturally.

Think of your networking connections as budding friendships with a business-centered purpose. And don't expect every interaction to result in some defined outcome. You might even find, over time, that your networking partners develop into good friends as you share intimacies and work toward a professional goal from which you'll both benefit.

DOS AND DON'TS

Do: Make an emotional commitment to networking so that it becomes an integral part of your life.

Do: Be realistic in making networking commitments that you can and will keep.

Do: Plan your networking work, then work your plan.

Do: Be focused and decisive in getting your networking tasks done.

Do: Try to get most of your networking activities finished during the work day.

Do: Keep your priorities straight.

Do: Treat networking relationships like budding friendships.

Don't: Wait until you have time to network because you probably never will.

Don't: Think of your networking and your job as separate activities.

Don't: Fail to deliver when someone is depending on you.

Don't: Bring a lot of networking tasks home with you.

PRINCIPLE #3:
CULTIVATE BOTH
CONTACTS AND
CONNECTIONS

Anne, the development director of an educational film company, is identifying individuals who might serve on her firm's board of directors. She decides to consult with a few of her networking partners to get referrals, so she calls Paula, Dennis, and Maggie to set up lunch dates and asks them to think about possible candidates. She's been meaning to get in touch with each of them anyway and this way she can catch up with what's going on as well as get some suggestions for the board.

Michael, an architect, realizes that his rapidly growing firm needs to hire an office manager. He goes through his Rolodex one morning and by noon has called a dozen networking partners and industry contacts to get the word out and see if anyone can recommend candidates for the job.

In the first scenario, Anne takes a highly personalized approach, deliberately selecting certain networking partners who she thinks are most likely to know the kind of people she wants to consider for her firm's board. She sets up a situation in which her networking request will be presented in a social context that will allow her to deepen her relationship with each of her partners.

Michael takes a much different approach, contacting several people with a focused, immediate objective. While each of his phone calls might include a brief catch-up exchange, his primary purpose is to make sure his partners are alerted to his immediate need.

Whose networking approach is better? Neither. While Anne and Michael are networking differently, each will probably get what he or she needs. But both could be even more successful by learning from each other's techniques.

Anne's approach focuses on making *connections*, concentrating her networking energies on building long-term relationships with a few key people. Michael's method is to make *contacts*, touching base with various people whenever he has a particular need. The trick to really successful networking is to do both: go for depth as well as breadth, making plenty of connections as well as contacts.

In my many years of networking, I've observed that, more often than not, women tend to make connections, while men are more likely to make contacts. Let's take a minute to examine why men and women approach networking—like so many other things—differently.

A lot of research is being conducted on how women and men develop patterns of interaction. One study became the basis of a best-selling book, *You Just Don't Understand* (Ballantine Books, 1991), by Dr. Deborah Tannen, a professor of linguistics at Georgetown University. In tracing the socialization of boys and girls, Dr. Tannen points out that we start developing distinct ways of interacting with our friends during childhood. Girls play in small groups or pairs where intimacy is key and the center of their social life is a best friend. In games and other activities, rules are flexible, negotiable, and changed by group process. Boys' activities and games are hierarchically structured, with a leader who tells others what to do. Their activities have winners and losers and elaborate systems of rules.

Although each individual is unique and no generalization will apply to every case, it seems that the patterns we developed in childhood continue to operate for many of us as adults. The implication is that women are oriented toward one-on-one, interpersonal relationships, while men get along with each other to achieve individual and group goals in the interest of team spirit.

Now that we understand where we're coming from, let's see where we can go. I believe that if you want to enhance your networking effectiveness, you have to cultivate both contacts *and* connections. You have to interact with a number of different people to expand your pool of networking contacts; and you have to deepen your relationships with particularly promising people to make them networking connections.

MAKING CONTACTS

When it comes to networking, quantity as well as quality counts. The more people you welcome into your networking circle, the better your chances of success because the odds are in your favor. So as you meet, greet, and exchange information with the many people who move in and out of your life every day, consider each of them a possible networking contact. Develop casual yet cordial relationships with those individuals who you think might be able to help you reach your professional or personal goals—and vice versa. You may not be calling on these people right now, but you want to keep the link intact in case you ever want to ask for their help.

To increase the number and variety of networking contacts you make, join groups that give you a chance to meet people both inside and outside of your industry. Attend several meetings to meet some members and get a feel for the group. And by all means look over the membership list to see that those involved are in positions to complement your networking goals and that you have something to offer to them in return.

Broaden Your Contact Base Through Joining . . .

Industry trade associations
Business lunch clubs
Self-improvement clubs like Toastmasters International
Alumni groups
Charitable organizations
Community groups
Social clubs

You can also attract promising networking contacts to *you* by raising your visibility. For example, you can:

- Run for office, either in an organization you belong to or in your community.
- Become an industry spokesperson in your area of expertise.
- Get appointed to committees and task forces within your company and industry.
- Edit or write articles for industry journals and newsletters.

MAKING CONNECTIONS

In addition to casting a wide net that encompasses many casual networking contacts, you'll want to have some deeper and richer long-term networking relationships with selected individuals. These personal, high-quality connections, based on genuine interest and concern between partners, often evolve into friendships. The partners usually share a strong level of trust and honesty, which makes their interaction straightforward and satisfying.

Learn to Connect By . . .

Tutoring adults or children.
Acting as a mentor to a promising fellow professional.
Serving as a "big brother" or "big sister" to a young person.
Volunteering in a hospice, soup kitchen, or elderly care facility.

Learning how to connect with others in lasting ways can make networking a personally enjoyable and rewarding experience. Developing solid connections helps you build loyalty, trust, and intimacy with your partners, giving you a valuable sounding board for talking about ideas and matters that are important to you. It also encourages truly involved and committed relationships that take networking to a whole different level of interaction.

I'm not suggesting that you make every networking partner your best buddy. Selectivity is the key here. From your circle of contacts, zero in on at least three individuals you feel you could build a close one-on-one relationship with. Look for people with whom you share common interests, concerns, and activities that could form the basis of a nonbusiness social acquaintance—and maybe even a close personal friendship.

As you know from your personal relationships, it takes time to get close to another person. So don't expect too much too soon. The first step is to add a social dimension to your relationship. When you get together for a career-related networking meeting, for instance, talk about personal interests as well instead of keeping the whole conversation anchored in business. If you both follow a certain sports team or enjoy the same cultural activity, suggest getting together for the next game or performance. Once your relationship has evolved to the level where you socialize comfortably together, you've paved the way to deepening it even further, if you choose.

When you're interested in making networking connections, it helps to nurture the attitudes and skills you need to do that successfully. So it may be valuable to join organizations or engage in activities that encourage the kind of one-on-one or small group involvement that breaks down barriers between people.

It may take an effort to overcome any reservations you have about opening up to a professional networking partner. But your self-consciousness will soon pass and you may find that you're making a profound change in your personal as well as professional life.

LEARNING FROM OTHERS

The best way to learn about making contacts and connections is, of course, to seek out potential networking partners who are adept at either—or both—of these approaches. Talk about your networking goals and techniques and ask for advice. As always, be cautious in choosing your networking partners. You not only have to respect each other as professionals but also must feel that your personal styles are compatible so that you feel comfortable incorporating your partner's techniques into your networking pattern. If this isn't the case, keep looking until you find the right person to learn from.

DOS AND DON'TS

Do: Go for both breadth and depth in your networking rela-
    tionships.

Do: Increase the number and variety of contacts you make.

Do: Develop deeper, lasting connections with selected part-
    ners.

Don't: Expect too much too soon when nurturing connections.

Don't: Let your initial discomfort at trying a different approach
       stop you from mastering it.

Don't: Try to duplicate the networking techniques of someone
       who doesn't share your personal style—adopt the ones
       you can be comfortable with.

PRINCIPLE #4: APPROACH THE RIGHT PARTNER WITH THE RIGHT REQUEST

Here's the situation: Alexandra and Fred are salespeople having a networking lunch. After Fred talks about what he's been doing, Alex says:

a) **"Since companies you call on regularly could use my skills, why don't you keep your eyes open for me?"**

b) **"Keep me in mind."**

c) **"Of the companies you mentioned, Finn Brothers, Franklin Corporation, and A.B. Morehouse are places where I'd like to get my foot in the door. Could you introduce me to their production managers when you visit them?"**

It's easy to get carried away with enthusiasm for your networking plan and end up asking too much or too little from your networking partners. Either extreme can spell disaster to the relationship. If you ask too much, you risk turning off your networking partners because they resent being asked to spend more time and energy on your priorities than they feel is justified. When you ask too little, your request isn't viewed as serious or important and simply doesn't establish a priority in the other person's mind—or your own.

Let's review the three comments above to see how appropriate they are.

a) This request is asking too much. It implies that as Fred works his territory he should be watching out for Alex's priorities as well. Fred has enough to do just managing his own business without scouting for Alex.

b) A comment as vague and unstructured as this doesn't even sound like a serious request. It's just an offhanded remark that is easy to dismiss.

c) Bingo! Here is a specific and focused request. Fred may say no because he has other priorities. But at least it's a clear request that he can act on if he thinks it's appropriate.

A good way to judge what's "just right" to ask for is to write down the actions a referral resource will have to take in order to network effectively on your behalf. Then, as objectively as possible, ask yourself, "If I were in the other person's shoes, how would I respond to this request?" Do your homework before asking for a favor. Know your networking partner well enough to understand his or her priorities, needs, pressures, and contact opportunities so that you can gauge whether or not you're asking for something realistic.

Think about what you've learned about the other person based on the guidelines I suggested in the chapter on "Making Connections." Analyze the professional, personal, social, and networking behaviors and styles of the individual you want to approach to see how they fit with what you need right now. How does your need for networking support complement your partner's:

- Professional strengths?
- Industry expertise?
- Job-related projects and work habits?
- Need for personal payoff?
- Networking goals and methods?
- Scope and usual types of networking partners?

- Networking style and results orientation?

Does your request for help complement your partner's personal and social goals, such as:

- Professional and social club memberships?
- Community and cultural priorities?
- Political values, goals, and activities?

The more areas in which you can find a match between what you need and what your networking partner would be likely to do because it complements his or her own priorities, the more willing support you're apt to get. If you end up with no or very few matches, you probably would be asking too much of that particular person. Go through the same process with your other networking partners until you find a person whose background and interests complement your

---

Planning Your Approach

1. Develop a simple, focused networking strategy. It should be brief and concise, with no more than three to five key points.
2. Compare and contrast your strategy with the goals, aspirations, and needs of your networking partners. Look for the best fit. Then talk with the partners most closely aligned with your needs.
3. Outline your plan to your partners and explain how your skills could be useful to their networking contacts.
4. List specific people, companies, associations, and groups you'd like access to so that your networking partner has an action plan to go by. Make it easy for him or her to say, "Who do I know in this organization (or on this list) who might be helpful?" This focused approach shows that you respect your partner's valuable time.

needs. That's the person to approach with this particular networking request.

It also helps to get a reality check by consulting a close friend. Brief your friend on what you know about your referral resource and what you want the person to do, then get his or her frank opinion. Are you being realistic? Should you scale back your request? Would it be better to try someone else?

There's a practical advantage to testing your networking plan objectively. Good networking partners are precious resources and you don't want to undermine a good relationship by being overly self-centered when asking for assistance. Time is just as rare a commodity for your networking partner as it is for you so be sparing in your use of it. Be thoughtful in asking the right favor from the right person. Essentially, what you want to do is engineer win-win relationships with all of your networking partners.

To show you how to use these guidelines in approaching the appropriate networking partner with a realistic request, here are a few scenes enacting a situation related to a specific networking goal.

"Bruce Cassidy and the Sundak Kid"

The Characters

Noriko Hirose (The Networker) is the research and marketing development manager for Sundak Corporation, a respected biotechnology company. A bright, talented, and ambitious young woman, she wants to become recognized as an industry leader among biotechnology companies as well as federal and state government entities responsible for funding and favorable legislation.

Bruce Cassidy (The Networking Partner) is the research director of a biotechnology company that isn't a direct competitor of Sundak. He's a brilliant, esteemed researcher, widely regarded as one of the key promoters of biotechnology since the industry's start-up about 25 years ago. Although he's made many contacts inside and outside his specialized field, Bruce doesn't use them for personal or company gain but rather to advance the industry. He has worked to promote industry positions, circulating favorable industry information to strengthen funding requests and to gain popular support for biotech initiatives. He is a charter member of many key associations but feels most comfortable keeping a low profile. Bruce is quite willing to assist others with industry and personal agendas, and he has helped a number of people and their companies attain high visibility. He is especially interested in helping networking partners who are willing to tackle difficult yet rewarding legislation and funding opportunities.

Scene 1

Noriko and Bruce meet at an industry luncheon. Since she recognizes his name and is intrigued by his views, she subsequently learns as much as she can about his background. Realizing that she and Bruce share similar values about the industry and its future, Noriko fashions the following strategy to support her long-range goal of being viewed as an industry leader:

1. Start working with key people inside and outside the industry to advance legislation and funding resources for industry research and development.
2. Actively work toward being a spokesperson for key associations and become a member of key committees promoting change.
3. Become sought after as a speaker on issues of importance to the industry and thereby reach key business, scientific, and political forums.
4. Be invited into the inner circle of industry leaders who make changes that benefit the industry.

Scene 2

Considering the depth and breadth of Bruce's associations inside and outside the industry, he could influence just about any initiative a networker might desire. But Noriko decides to approach him with this particular strategy because it dovetails with Bruce's priority of championing the industry. She figures that Bruce will be more willing to network aggressively on her behalf for this objective than for a more personally directed goal. And she's playing into his strengths because he knows many of the people she wants to meet.

Scene 3

Now that Noriko has matched her networking strategy to Bruce's desires and abilities, she invites him to lunch to discuss her plan and how they might work together. After outlining the four elements of her strategy, she asks for Bruce's advice about next steps.

Bruce, delighted that someone else is willing to share the responsibility for moving industry priorities forward, explains his own public interest networking agenda to Noriko. Together, they develop a joint strategy to go after the key players influencing and making decisions at the state and federal levels, to cultivate important industry insiders to gain support for legislation and funding initiatives, and to develop additional synergy among industry and association members to influence others inside and outside the field. Bruce sees himself as the behind-the-scenes architect planning strategy, with Noriko playing a more public role. He plans to introduce her to well-placed state and federal officials and, at her request, agrees to arrange meetings with influential industry insiders to generate grassroots support.

Epilogue

Noriko ends up getting two of her four needs satisfied from the start (networking inside and outside the industry and meeting the inner circle leaders) because she initially focuses on priorities that Bruce favors. Because their goals are so compatible, Bruce is willing—even eager—to work hard to help Noriko succeed. She's also well positioned to accomplish the other two points of her strategy (becoming a spokesperson for key associations and being sought after as a speaker on important issues) as she expands her state and local government contacts and moves into the inner circle of the industry.

This networking connection certainly helps Noriko, but what does Bruce, who is doing the favors, get out of it? Because Bruce is more altruistic than self-focused in his networking goals, he gains satisfaction from seeing his initiatives benefit the industry being supported and popularized by someone besides himself. And he might even see in Noriko a protege who will carry the torch in the years to come.

The End

Like Noriko, you have to be street smart when you plan your networking strategy. You need to match up your different goals with those people who can do the most to help you achieve them because they relate to their own priorities. This might mean that you have to temporarily delay working toward some goals you aspire to as you initially allow the priorities of others to dictate your agenda. But it can all work out for you in time if you're willing to be patient and let the natural synergy of networking operate to get what you want.

DOS AND DON'TS

Do: Think about what kind of effort it will take for a partner to help you before making a request.

Do: Match specific requests to the capabilities and needs of particular networking partners.

Do: Be thoughtful and appropriate in asking for help from networking partners.

Don't: Ask too much or too little of your networking partners.

Don't: Make vague, undefined requests for assistance which require your partner to do your thinking for you.

PRINCIPLE #5: DO FOR OTHERS AS THEY DO FOR YOU

The Golden Rule of Reciprocity dictates that you do for others as they do for you. Nothing kills networking relationships faster than a user mentality. If you make a habit out of taking without giving much back, most of your networking partners will be too polite to say, "What have you done for me lately?" They will just as politely find every excuse in the book not to have anything more to do with you.

Networking is not about going through as many contacts as you can, using them for what you need at the moment and then moving on to the next target. As we've discussed, networking is a lifelong pursuit with long-term partners, and it's the quality of your involvement with others—your respect for them and responsiveness to their needs—that creates a good networking relationship.

This goes far beyond asking for and returning specific requests for assistance. In a good networking relationship, your partner is out there promoting your interests, looking for appropriate referrals, and scouting out opportunities that would be right for you. So that means you have to be every bit as aggressive in promoting his or her interests. You'd be surprised at how naturally this happens as you keep cross-fertilizing your work, your networking, your referral contacts, and your business opportunities. You just have to keep reminding yourself that one of your networking tasks is to make things happen for your networking partners.

Making Things Happen

Introduce your networking partners to people they would
    benefit from meeting.
Look for opportunities to increase your partners' visibility.
Suggest new networking ideas for your partners to try.
Generate cross-networking opportunities among your partners.

INTRODUCE YOUR NETWORKING PARTNERS TO PEOPLE THEY WOULD BENEFIT FROM MEETING

If you think it would help one of your networking partners to meet someone else you know—a business colleague, an association or club member, a social friend or acquaintance—then do what you can to get them together. Explain to both parties why you think there would be value in their meeting each other. If they're interested, host a lunch, dinner, or some other occasion where they can get acquainted in a relaxed atmosphere. After you've made the introductions, step back and let their relationship take its course.

By helping your partner in this way, you might also end up helping yourself. Assuming, of course, that the meeting is a fruitful one for the individuals involved, this approach is likely to win you the gratitude of both parties, enhance your value as a well-connected person, and increase their perceptions of your interpersonal skills.

In some cases, there's an added possibility of gain for you. Maybe the person you're introducing your partner to is someone you'd like to cultivate yourself, but at this point you don't feel there's anything you could bring to the relationship. You can see that your partner's background and experience make for a much better initial fit with that person. And, in time, your partner may be able to pave the way for you to deepen your own relationship with the person. The story of Jim and Tony will show you how this works.

> *The Networkers:* Jim, a freelance computer programmer, and Tony, the technical support manager at Microdesign, a software company for which Jim has done some work.
>
> *The Situation:* At his weekly aerobics class, Jim struck up an acquaintance with Trisha, the chief financial officer at a large insurance company that could be a source of business for him. Trisha mentioned that she needed to upgrade the computer system used by her staff.
>
> *The Action:* Jim arranged for Trisha to meet with Tony, whose company specializes in creating customized systems.
>
> *The Outcome:* Trisha got the system she needed. Tony made points with his boss for bringing business into Microdesign. Jim was hired by Tony to program Trisha's system. Since this gave Jim the chance to demonstrate his professional skills to Trisha, he could feel comfortable asking her to refer him to managers in other parts of the company who might be able to use his services.

A word of caution about these kinds of situations. Don't presume that because you've made the connection between two people you've earned special privileges. Jim, for example, didn't feel that Tony was obligated to hire him to work on Trisha's program (although Tony, grateful for the referral, did so because Jim was qualified to handle the project). And Jim didn't assume that Trisha would refer him to others just because he helped her solve a problem. He had to prove his professional capabilities to earn her respect and confidence. Remember that your prime objective here is not personal gain, but rather the promotion of your networking partner. Of course, you hope that somehow you'll benefit as well. But that's not the reason you're doing it.

LOOK FOR OPPORTUNITIES TO INCREASE THE VISIBILITY OF YOUR NETWORKING PARTNERS

As a dedicated networker, you're constantly striving to be visible and well known to people inside and outside your business environment. As your efforts lead to opportunities for yourself, also be on the lookout for opportunities for your networking partners. If you belong to the same professional organization as Partner A, for example, nominate her for office (with her prior consent, of course). If Partner B, who works in a related field to yours, is an articulate speaker, try to get him on the program of the next conference you're involved in. If you're active in a charitable organization that also appeals to Partner C, work to have her named to head a fund-raising committee.

Take, for example, Kate, a consultant specializing in "green" (environmentally friendly) merchandising. One of her clients—and networking partners—is Amal, a vice president of marketing at a major consumer products firm who has mounted an aggressive campaign to make his company's product packaging ecologically sound. For the past few years, Kate has been teaching a marketing course in the continuing education division of a noted university in her city, and she's had Amal come in to speak to her classes as a guest lecturer. Because of other commitments, Kate won't be able to teach the class next semester and suggests that Amal replace her. He turns out to be terrific in the classroom and the division administrator asks him to stay on the faculty to teach another course after Kate's return. As a result of this referral, Kate makes double networking points: Amal won't forget the effort she made in getting him this exposure; and the administrator has another reason to appreciate Kate's contributions to the university.

If your networking partner is better known than you are, you could benefit from the association, gaining stature among your peers in the organizations you bring him or her into. If you promote one of your networking partners for a public engagement that not's right for you, the chances are that he or she will return the courtesy by recommending you for situations where you would be qualified. Helping your networking partners create a higher public profile also puts you in networking contact with movers and shakers in various groups and associations who appreciate creative ideas that can boost their success. And that opens up a whole new set of possibilities for you.

SUGGEST NEW NETWORKING IDEAS FOR YOUR PARTNERS

While you and your fellow networkers are very busy people with your own jobs, careers, networking priorities, and next steps, you can develop incredible synergy if you help your partners look for other networking opportunities. The idea is to identify networking avenues that your partner has not yet tried but that you think would be effective for him or her. This technique works best for high-energy networkers who are willing to make the investment of extra time and energy required.

The process is simple: Considering the other person's networking goals and strategies, put yourself in his or her place and ask yourself, "What would be my next steps?"

To illustrate this example, let's go back to Noriko, the research and marketing development manager at Sundak, and her networking partner Bruce, the research director of another biotechnology company, whom we met in "Principle #4: Approach the Right Partner with the Right Request." Noriko knows that Bruce is considered a "founding father" of biotechnology. He's a low-key guy who works tirelessly to promote industry goals but is reluctant to push his own agenda. Noriko has noticed that health care is taking center stage as a subject of national concern and she sees an opportunity for Bruce.

Since biotech applications are likely to play a significant role as the health-care agenda unfolds, Noriko thinks he could bring a great deal of knowledge and experience to the public debate. She figures that Bruce might find it intriguing to form and lead a blue ribbon panel to advise government entities, such as the National Institutes of Health, on major policy issues in the health-care area. As his networking partner, she broaches the idea with him. Bruce decides to act on it, feeling that he could make a significant contribution to the industry and the country. The situation could also open up a new vista of networking opportunities for Bruce and his trusted networking partners—including Noriko.

GENERATE CROSS-NETWORKING OPPORTUNITIES AMONG YOUR PARTNERS

The concept that "the whole is greater than the sum of its parts" is certainly true when it comes to networking. Productive group activity somehow can unleash creative energy that leads to new ideas, directions, and results. If you think that nurturing good individual networking relationships can be powerful, wait till you see what happens when you combine the energies of multiple networking partners.

Once you've developed trusting, productive relationships with your different partners, figure out how to use the synergy you have with each of them in ways that can benefit them as a larger group. Invite compatible partners to meet with you to trade ideas on how the group, working together, can make the most out of its collective networking relationships.

Before the meeting, prepare brief biographies of each participant that focus on individual networking priorities, significant skills and experience, and areas of special interest. Circulate the biographies in advance so that everyone has a chance to review them, and ask each person to come to the meeting prepared with ideas concerning:

1. *Opportunities for personal gain.* In what ways could I interact with other people here for mutual benefit? Could I help anyone by introducing them to people I know? Do I see possible connections between other individuals in the group?

2. *A group project directed toward a larger goal.* Is there a way that all, or a significant number, of us could pool our talents and contacts in an effort for the "greater good," such as setting up a food bank for the needy in our community or raising funds for a local cultural organization?

Setting up a "greater good" project serves a number of purposes. First, of course, it uses the considerable talents and skills of the group to provide help to those who need it. It also gives individuals a chance to make a substantial contribution to a worthwhile cause that they don't feel they have the time or energy to commit to on their own. And the group gains experience in working together in an area of common interest.

Even if the group isn't interested in supporting a common goal at this time, participants will become aware of the power they command if they should choose to combine their resources at a later date. In addition, the group meeting can lead to one-to-one networking liaisons that might not have taken place if you hadn't made the effort. And there's added value for you in that you demonstrate your leadership and vision by making the most of your networking relationships for yourself as well as your partners.

Whether you're out there promoting individual networking partners or fostering group synergy, you're being a good networker by nourishing your relationships to keep them vital and productive.

DOS AND DON'TS

Do: Be out there making things happen for your networking partners.

Do: Consider whether any of your networking partners could benefit from meeting other people in your business, social, and personal circles.

Do: Recommend your networking partners for appropriate high-profile public engagements.

Do: Try to promote group synergy among your networking partners.

Don't: Think that your networking job is done simply by returning a favor for a partner.

Don't: Hesitate to suggest a good networking idea that you think would be right for a particular partner.

Don't: Assume that by bringing two people together you earn any special status in their relationship.

PRINCIPLE #6: GO THE EXTRA MILE FOR YOUR NETWORKING PARTNERS

Karen is a financial analyst ready to make the move to a new position with more responsibility. She's preparing for a meeting with her new networking partner Fran, who heads an up-and-coming venture capital firm and knows everybody in the financial community. Karen prepares a solid capabilities briefing that details her education, experience, skills, and strengths that she plans to give to Fran in the hope of being referred to some of the industry people Fran knows.

By putting together a comprehensive professional portrait of herself, Karen is being a thoughtful and proactive networking partner—up to a point. But what she's not doing is going that extra mile that will make it easier for Fran to assist her—and will impress Fran with her focus and savvy.

Going the extra mile means figuring out ways to help your networking partner help you. It means "connecting the dots" for the other person so that he or she doesn't have to make a major effort deciding when and how to refer you. And it also means showing your appreciation for your partner's help by finding a way to do something extra for him or her.

Karen would be going the extra mile by giving Fran the names of the firms she would most like to work for and the executives she would like to meet in those and other companies. It would also help if she specified precisely what she wanted from those encounters—for example, to apply for a particular job opening, to arrange an informational interview, or to cultivate additional networking partners.

Karen made a mistake common to many beginning networkers. "Fran is smart and well-connected," she reasoned. "She'll have a better sense than I would about how best to use the information I've given her. Besides, I don't want to offend or bore her by getting into too much detail about the kind of job I want. I'll be glad for any suggestions she can give me."

This argument, while perfectly logical, is also perfectly wrong.

Look at it from Fran's perspective. She's carrying a lot of responsibility running a young company and is too busy with her own priorities to expend a lot of time and energy promoting Karen's cause. So if Karen fails to let Fran know precisely what she's looking for, Fran may not have the time or motivation to do it herself or may not come up with the referrals that will help Karen most. But if Fran is given some key points that help her match Karen's capabilities and strengths with her own business acquaintances' needs and priorities, it becomes much easier for her to network on Karen's behalf.

Every networking situation is different, of course, and you have to be thoughtful and creative in finding that unique way in which you can go "above and beyond" for your partner in each particular encounter.

Accruing Mileage

- Give your partners specific guidance about areas in which your skills and abilities would be valuable to their contacts.
- Develop a list of companies and key people you're interested in so that your partners have a clear picture of what kinds of referrals are most useful to you.
- Identify specific types of people who could benefit from meeting you.
- Find something special you can do for your partner.

GIVE YOUR NETWORKING PARTNERS SPECIFIC GUIDANCE ABOUT AREAS IN WHICH YOUR SKILLS AND ABILITIES WOULD BE VALUABLE TO THEIR CONTACTS

When your networking partners have a handle on your areas of expertise, they'll be able to refer you immediately when they run into a contact who needs what you have to offer. If you're a lawyer, for instance, explain to all of your networking partners the focus and scope of your practice, including information about typical cases you would handle, the kind of clients you usually take on, and the way you work with clients to solve problems and provide the advice they need.

Here's an actual example of how this approach can yield results. When my wife and I were at our real estate lawyer's office signing the blizzard of papers to refinance our home mortgage, I mentioned in passing that a friend of ours had been fired from his job recently and suspected that age discrimination had been a key reason. I asked our attorney if he knew of a good human resources lawyer. Without missing a beat, he scrawled the name of an outstanding specialist on his business card, then wrapped up the exchange with this caveat: If our friend ended up contacting the human resources lawyer, he wanted our friend to mention him as the referral source so that he would get networking credit.

When describing your capabilities to a partner, be confident in the way you represent yourself, but also be honest about your level of experience and ability. This is not the time to exaggerate. You don't want to embarrass your partners by having them recommend you in good faith and later hear that you had misrepresented your qualifications. On the other hand, you shouldn't be shy or self-effacing. If you haven't had a particular experience but believe that you have transferable skills that would enable you to do that kind of job well, let your networking partner know.

DEVELOP A LIST OF COMPANIES AND KEY PEOPLE YOU'RE INTERESTED IN SO THAT YOUR NETWORKING PARTNERS HAVE A CLEAR PICTURE OF WHAT KINDS OF REFERRALS ARE MOST USEFUL TO YOU

Be very specific about what it is you're looking for. The more precise you are, the more focused your partner can be in making referrals for you. Let's go back to our friend Karen. Karen starts making her list for Fran and begins with "banks." What banks? "First International." This bank has offices around the world. In what city or region of the country or the world would she be willing to work? What area or division does she want to work in? What are the names and titles of the people she would like to meet? These are the kinds of questions Karen needs to ask herself to get down to specifics. Then she would repeat this process with every company she lists.

In this as in any situation, submitting a detailed list doesn't mean that your referral resources will necessarily be able to put you in touch with the right people right away. But they're always enlarging their base of acquaintances so they may be able to make a connection for you in the future. And sometimes they may not be able to connect you directly with the person you want to meet but can introduce you to someone who can. Fran, for example, doesn't know the vice president of research at First International Bank who is at the top of Karen's list. She does, however, know that one of her acquaintances, Chris, used to work for him. So she agrees to introduce Karen to Chris. At this point, Fran is out of the loop and it's up to Karen to take the matter further with Chris.

IDENTIFY SPECIFIC TYPES OF PEOPLE WHO COULD BENEFIT FROM MEETING YOU

Spell out for your networking partners the kinds of people who could use your services or gain something from being associated with you. This is especially important if your partners only know certain aspects of your work or associate you with one particular job or field. You might have a skill or ability that can be applied in many more areas than the one you've been working in. For example, a writer who has spent several years in an advertising agency needs to let her partners know that graphic designers and public relations firms could also use her services.

In some cases, your networking partners can team you up with people who need you as much as you need them to get a particular project off the ground. Here's how one school board member used his network this way:

The school board Len sits on realized that it needed special equipment and training to prepare high school students for the job market but didn't have the money to implement the project. Len figured that since companies in the region would benefit from having a well-trained pool of potential employees, they might be willing to fund the training. So he networked with local business-people, asking for specific referrals to decision-makers at companies within a 50-mile radius of the school district. He personally met with each one of these decision-makers to discuss and establish a working relationship that wound up meeting the needs of both the school board and the businesses.

FIND SOMETHING SPECIAL YOU CAN DO FOR YOUR NETWORKING PARTNERS

Although most networking relationships are between equals, there are times when one party stands to gain more from the process than the other. Sometimes you attract a networking partner who has much better contacts than you do right now and at first glance seems to be offering you a lot more than you can offer him or her. If you're in this situation, it's wise to demonstrate your appreciation to the other person. You don't have to call attention to the imbalance, but you should find ways to even the score. What do you have to give back? Your creativity, energy, and enthusiasm.

Let's see how this played out for Karen and Fran:

> In the course of their conversation, Karen discovered that Fran is deeply committed to bringing cultural arts programs to the public schools in the city where they live. The local school board, however, had put all cultural initiatives on the back burner because of budget problems. Even though Karen isn't particularly interested in getting performing arts programs into the schools, she realized she might be able to help Fran's cause—and schoolchildren as well—by using her skills and contacts to research the situation for Fran and come up with some options, such as corporate funding, to get the plan moving forward.

With this approach, Karen earned Fran's respect for being so resourceful and considerate. What Karen lacked in depth and breadth of contacts to network effectively for Fran was offset by her energy and creativity in helping Fran solve a problem that was frustrating her. This type of cooperative synergy ends up as a win-win for everyone.

DOS AND DON'TS

Do: "Connect the dots" for your networking partners to make it easy for them to refer you.

Do: Be confident but honest in telling your partners about your skills and experience.

Do: Be specific about what you want for yourself and from your partner.

Don't: Assume that your networking partners automatically know how to use the information you give them.

Don't: Get discouraged if your partners can't help you right away—they may be able to do something for you down the line.

Don't: Forget to show your appreciation for a partner's help.

PRINCIPLE #7:
CELEBRATE SUCCESS

Congratulations! Well done. Nice job. Way to go.

Get used to saying these words to your networking partners, and to hearing them in return, because you deserve to give yourself and others some credit for your networking triumphs.

Celebrating success is the networking principle that most people forget to adopt. Since networking is just one of the many things you and your partners are doing every day, it's easy to lose sight of the progress you've made, individually and together. Yet it's important to recognize and celebrate your networking achievements and give your self-esteem a well-deserved boost. You get some kind of rewards from your work—starting with your paycheck and hopefully extending to things like management recognition, bonuses, and promotions as well. But you also devote a lot of talent, energy, and dedication to your networking projects. And somehow you need to get back something beyond your own sense of satisfaction to keep you committed to your networking activities.

Maybe achievers like you think you have enough in the self-esteem department. But I believe that you, like everyone else, need validation that what you and your networking partners do, and how you do it, has value.

In *The Psychology of Self-Esteem* (J. P. Tarcher, 1980), psychologist Dr. Nathaniel Braden defines self-esteem as the sum of self-confidence and self-respect. He explains that external validation of your thoughts about yourself can be a major source of self-esteem. If your only input comes from your own perception of the job you're doing, there's always room for self-doubt. Am I doing enough? Too much? Am I doing it right? Am I missing something? Is this what others want? Am I using my time well? Could others do the job better? Validation from others that says you're doing just fine—and maybe even better than that—is a "reality check" that gives you a more balanced view of yourself.

Dr. B. David Brooks, in his book *A Self-Esteem Repair and Maintenance Manual* (Kincaid House, 1990), says it simply: "Attitude leads to action, leads to achievement, which when acknowledged, leads to higher self-esteem." What this means to me is that achievers get energized through the validation of their efforts. This is why celebrating success is so important for networkers.

Revel in your Success
Take stock of your achievements. Celebrate with your networking partners. Share with friends and family. Look to others for inspiration.

TAKE STOCK OF YOUR ACHIEVEMENTS

The first step you need to take toward celebrating your successes is identifying your achievements. Periodically take stock of yourself and honestly assess the positive contributions to your job, career, and personal life that you've made through networking. These can be measurable accomplishments, such as setting up a networking lunch date or calling a referral. Or they can be positive qualities you've demonstrated, like managing your time more efficiently or improving your interpersonal skills. Make a list and put it up where you can refer to it frequently as an inspiration.

If you sometimes find that you don't have anything to put on the list, that's O.K. You've probably earned a rest. But if too much time passes, or you're having a lot of trouble developing your list, maybe you're being too hard on yourself in defining what a worthwhile accomplishment is. Talk it over with someone close to you who may be able see your achievements more clearly and objectively than you can.

Once you've taken stock of your recent triumphs, share your successes with people important to you. You'll feel good and—if you do it right—they will too.

CELEBRATE SUCCESS WITH YOUR NETWORKING PARTNERS

You don't have to throw a party, but you do have to acknowledge to your networking partners that their intervention on your behalf has paid off. What constitutes an appropriate way of saying "thanks" will vary from partner to partner. For some people, a simple explanation of the result is thanks enough. Others consider being taken to lunch a gracious gesture. And still others feel generously rewarded if you can engineer a quick payback by following through on a networking priority of theirs. Personalize your approach to show each of your networking partners that you understand his or her individual need for adequate recognition.

Since networking efforts often take time to develop and nurture to the point of paying off, remember to acknowledge your partners' ongoing efforts on your behalf as well as thank them for the results. When you recognize and reward the help of your networking partners, you demonstrate that you value their support and desire their continued involvement in the future.

SHARE WITH FRIENDS AND FAMILY

Some people may hesitate to tell friends and colleagues about efforts they're proud of because they don't want to come across as being boastful. You shouldn't let this fear stop you from sharing your much deserved satisfaction for a job well done. The fact is, how the information is received depends on how you present it. You can be direct and factual in relating and celebrating your personal success without showing off.

I have a friend who once taught me an important lesson about how to express appropriate self-pride without going over the line into bombast. He had been a major in the Marine Corps and served as Secretary to the Joint Chiefs of Staff for many years. When I asked him how he had been chosen for that assignment, he replied unabashedly that it was because he was the best person for the job—he had two master's degrees, had graduated from both war colleges, was a line officer, and was adept at the politics of the military. Some might think my friend was boasting. But I felt he was simply celebrating himself and sharing this information with me in a nonthreatening manner that came from his having a secure and realistic sense of self. And one of the ways he gave me that impression was by keeping the conversation focused on the *facts* related to his Joint Chiefs assignment. He didn't have to embellish or interpret the information because the facts spoke loudly enough for themselves.

I've observed that many notable people who have been widely recognized for their achievements don't boast about them. Rather, they explain the value of their contribution by sharing personal examples of the pride, the results, and the gratification they've experienced that helped them to carry on.

Another way to celebrate your successes is to select a safe environment—with your family, for example, or with a group of friends who understand you well —and develop a mechanism for sharing good things that happen. Set aside some time every week, over lunch or dinner perhaps, and establish some ground rules. First, everyone has to share something good that happened that week. Second, each person should concentrate on relating just the facts surrounding the event (to ward off those nasty critters boast and bombast). And third, each should describe how he or she felt about the good experiences that took place. This approach couldn't be more simple and direct—or more effective.

LOOK TO OTHERS FOR INSPIRATION

As you learn to celebrate your successes, it helps to look to other successful people to inspire you. To underscore the power of self-esteem, the celebration of success, and the value of maintaining it, I'd like to leave you with a story about a man whose achievements are well known but whose personal battle to attain them isn't.

He is said to have written to a friend, "I am the most miserable man living. Whether I shall be better I cannot tell." And it's no wonder he was so discouraged. As a young man, he lost his job, was refused admission to law school, and watched several of his businesses fail. His political career almost didn't get off the ground as he lost election after election for local and state office. His personal life was a series of tragedies, including the death of the woman he loved, a sadly empty marriage, the death of a beloved son, and a nervous breakdown.

Despite the obstacles he had to overcome and the self-doubts that plagued him, he persevered. And at the age of 51 he became President of the United States. The man was Abraham Lincoln.

Self-esteem, which is fed by the celebration of worthwhile accomplishments, is a powerful force in each of us. Nurture yours and help it grow. It becomes you. And it becomes you!

DOS AND DON'TS

Do: Give yourself credit for your networking triumphs.

Do: Acknowledge your networking partners' ongoing efforts as well as thank them for results.

Do: Share your successes with those close to you.

Don't: Lose sight of the progress you've made, individually and with your partners.

Don't: Underestimate your need for validation from others to bolster your self-esteem.

Don't: Be afraid that talking about your achievements will be seen as boasting —just stick to the facts.

NETWORKING IN ACTION

Up, Down, and Across the Organization: Networking on the Job

Nobody in an organization has more enthusiasm for you, your career, your priorities, and your needs than you do. So you can be your own best promoter if you bring purpose, focus, and consistency to the task of building job capital within your company. The message you want to deliver to everyone—up, down, and across the organization—is that you're a valuable contributor, a team player with potential.

Networking within your organization can yield a number of benefits. It can enhance job performance as you and your partners help each other to be more efficient and effective. It can also gain you and your partners recognition from peers and managers as you identify and share ways to make your departments—and perhaps others—more productive.

How—and how much—you network on the job will probably relate to the networking styles I described in the chapter on "Developing Your Own Style." If you identified yourself as a laid-back or involved networker, you're likely to network as a situation arises.

Strategic or high-energy networkers, on the other hand, are much more proactive. Instead of waiting for an opportunity to present itself, they'll create one based on the company's larger directives and priorities.

Whatever kind of networker you are, if you're going to network effectively in your organization, you have to understand how that particular organization works. How is the company structured? How does one department's activities relate to the activities of others? What are the priorities of the people in those areas? Can they get things done that your department can't, and vice versa? Some sources you can consult to get this kind of information include annual reports, company product brochures, organizational charts and, of course, other employees.

In cultivating other employees, you want to cut across organizational lines to learn about what different people do and what impact doing certain things—and not doing them—has on the company. This means making an effort to meet individuals in other departments. You could ask someone you speak with frequently in the course of your work to join you for lunch one day. You can strike up conversations at the water cooler, on the coffee line, and at company functions. Or you can make it a point to sit with employees from other departments in the lounge or lunchroom. Exactly how you meet people depends on the circumstances of your job and company. But the idea is to be outgoing in making a number of different contacts and connections.

To understand why this is such a valuable approach, think a minute about how most organizations work. It's common for employees to interact most often and most comfortably with their immediate colleagues. If you're in human resources, for example, you tend to work, eat, and socialize with others on the human resources staff. Coworkers represent an affinity group whose members deal with the same kinds of problems and opportunities on a day-to-day basis.

You'll often find that even managers tend to be part of this affinity group, although they frequently interact with other departments in formal or informal ways.

Crossing departmental lines gives you an important advantage— you start to get a sense of the broader picture and see how things fit together. Not only will you learn more than most people in the company know about normal operations but you'll also gain insight about how things that work in one area can be applied to another.

So what do you do with all the information and ideas you pick up in your research and conversations? The idea is to share relevant information with a department (your own or another) that could use it to increase productivity. When you present the information, emphasize how it can benefit employees, the department, and even the company as a whole. This can inspire the person you're talking with to want change, plus give him or her good ammunition to initiate it.

By providing leadership in areas that aren't even your responsibility, over time you'll start to gain a reputation as a visionary with a wide-ranging interest in the company and the success of its people. You become known as someone who wants to make a difference and help others to make a difference, too. You also demonstrate that you're a good person to network with because you focus on mutual benefit.

As you begin your intracompany networking efforts, it will be important for you to find a comfort level in how and when you interact with your colleagues. See some ideas that could help smooth the way on page 120.

BE CURIOUS

Make it a point to get to know people in different areas of the company and to find out what they and their departments do. It can be an interesting and broadening experience.

BE A GOOD LISTENER

Ask good questions that get people talking about their departmental problems and opportunities. Learn how they operate, what frustrates them, what makes their jobs easier, how they get rewarded. Practice listening for what's being said between the lines so that you can work more effectively with them and perhaps help them to work more effectively with others.

Interacting at the Office

- Be curious.
- Be a good listener.
- If you have helpful ideas, think about how best to share them.
- Network at your own level to get a reputation as a team player before you network up in the organization.

IF YOU HAVE HELPFUL IDEAS, THINK ABOUT HOW BEST TO SHARE THEM

If you bluntly blurt out your ideas to others, you may come across as a know-it-all, which helps nobody. Put yourself in their shoes: what would they like to hear and how would they like to hear it to help them be more effective and useful? Let your contacts know that you're available, on an informal, unofficial basis, to help with next steps. Another good way to share your insights and skills is volunteering to join an interdepartmental or companywide team.

NETWORK AT YOUR OWN LEVEL TO GET A REPUTATION AS A TEAM PLAYER BEFORE YOU NETWORK UP IN THE ORGANIZATION

Set the groundwork for networking up in the company by first honing your networking skills and producing positive results with partners at or below your organizational level. Given the hierarchical structure of most organizations, you probably won't be in a position to approach someone at a higher level until you've become recognized fairly widely as an up-and-comer who has proven your value to the team. Then more opportunities should start coming your way.

I learned the value of networking up, down, and across the organization when I was the marketing manager in an operating division of a major foods products manufacturer. I was once working with someone in the Information Technology Group to develop a new client data base for my division. She commented that a problem in her department was that it had to produce too many reports. For example, for years it had been generating over 30 customized reports every month, quarter, and year for different sales offices. These special reports took up large amounts of computer space and processing time, but requests to reduce the output had received little attention from either headquarters or field sales management.

I was aware that both the marketing and sales departments had standard analysis and reporting procedures for forecasting and budgeting that field sales staff had to use. So I guessed that the special reports were now redundant. I discussed my observations with my friend in Information Technology and suggested that she contact several people I knew in the company who could find out (discreetly, of course) how the field people were using the special reports. As I suspected, the sales force didn't need them anymore and willingly gave them up when Information Technology explained that some of the information could be incorporated into the standardized reporting system. This move saved the Information Technology Group and the company considerable time, effort, and expense.

If the people in the Information Technology Group had pursued the sales reporting issue beyond official channels and learned more about how the information was being used, they would have arrived at the same conclusions I had. I didn't really go out of my way in this situation. I was simply curious about how things worked relative to my division.

Although Information Technology got rightful credit for streamlining the sales reporting system, I was associated with triggering change in the way that the company did things. My involvement became known up, down, and across the organization. This allowed me to network upward a level or two in the company because I was seen as a team player. For example, I later approached the design director, who was above my level, about helping him promote some interesting packaging concepts he liked that were outside the company's norm. Because I also knew the director of sales, I was able to help the design staff develop interest and support for the packaging from the sales force.

I'm not sure I could have networked up in the organization if I hadn't first developed a reputation as a good team player. Because I had done something that helped another department look good, the design and sales directors viewed me as a useful ally who could provide potential benefit for them.

Networking down in the organization is easy. People below your level are often looking for ways to be associated with success so that they, too, can be recognized. If you've established a reputation for having good ideas and sharing credit, people below your level are likely to feel comfortable approaching you with their ideas—and they're often brimming with them. If you can help them and yourself at the same time, you're likely to find these relationships to be very productive.

Now that you know the upside of networking within your organization, beware of the downside. First, don't get so busy networking that you let it infringe on your work. After all, the company is paying you to do your job, so make sure that you do it thoroughly and well. Second, remember to let your boss know what you're doing outside of the department. You don't want to be perceived as a threat, so keep your manager informed, and perhaps even involved, in your extradepartmental initiatives.

By networking inside your organization with sensitivity and genuine concern for the outcome, you can provide a valuable service that's sure to pay dividends down the road. Not only can you help to produce tangible results that help your company, but you also make connections up, down, and across the organization that will stand you in good stead in the future.

DOS AND DON'TS

Do: Deliver the message that you're a team player with potential.

Do: Learn how your organization works.

Do: Cultivate individuals outside of your own department.

Do: Share information that can help other departments be more productive.

Do: Keep your boss informed about your activities outside the department.

Don't: Neglect to make connections in all directions of your organization.

Don't: Come across as an obnoxious know-it-all when sharing information.

Don't: Network up in the organization until you're well-known as a team player.

Networking a Room: Using Social Settings

Which of the following is true for you?

As a dedicated networker, you go to a social event to:

a) **Meet potential networking partners.**

b) **Get out of the house on a Saturday night.**

c) **Enjoy yourself.**

The answer, of course, is all of the above. Any social occasion that brings together a diverse group of people—a friend's party, an alumni get-together at the theater, a neighbor's holiday open house, a charity event, a Chamber of Commerce meeting, an art gallery opening, a dinner cruise—presents an opportunity for you to network. Or, more accurately, for you to prepare to network. In a social setting, your goal as you meet people is simply to identify individuals as viable networking partners with whom you can follow up at a later date.

While a social event can provide fertile ground for networking, you don't have to take it so seriously that you forget your primary reason for being there: to have a good time. In fact, you don't have to network at all. There are times when you just want to go to some social gathering with no other agenda than to relax and enjoy yourself. You don't intend to network, you don't want to network, and you don't network.

But there are other occasions when you do want to meet and greet and network your heart out. Then the social event is an opportunity waiting to happen—but only if you plan for it. If you attend an event with some vague idea that maybe you'll meet someone who could be useful to your networking efforts down the road, chances are you and that person will pass like two ships in the night, never aware of each other's presence. To make sure that doesn't happen, consider taking this creative approach toward a social event.

Scenario for Successful Social Networking

- The Rehearsal: Assess the networking value of the event.
- The Performance: Demonstrate your character and competence.
- The Script: Ask questions to determine a person's potential as a networking partner.

THE REHEARSAL

The first thing you need to do is assess the networking value of the event. Namely, who's planning to attend? Many times you can find out by getting a guest or participant list ahead of time. Or, even better, ask friends or colleagues who have attended before. What kinds of people typically come to this event? Who did they meet? Who impressed them? Why?

Then, compare this information with your own networking agenda. Does meeting a particular individual at this event provide a stepping-stone to an organization you've been wanting to contact? Could anyone here help one of your networking partners? Would the meeting enhance your political or industry knowledge or help you with your job?

If your intelligence gathering indicates that the prospects are good, then go. If you're undecided, pass. Yes, I recognize that there's always the possibility of your meeting someone who would be a great connection. But that's true of any function you're invited to. And if you attend every one, you'll probably end up with little to show for your effort except less time than you have now, which means less time for networking. You have to manage your time and commitments better than that if you want to be successful. So my advice is to be a critical evaluator, choosing events that have visible and immediate potential and avoiding those with vague, undefined advantages.

THE PERFORMANCE

Now that you've decided to go, what do you want to do once you get there? In a primarily social situation, you have a unique opportunity to make a good impression on others and develop trust by demonstrating two key points about yourself: character and competence. So when you walk into the room, there are three things you want to accomplish:

- Enjoy yourself.
- Meet those key individuals who prompted you to attend the event in the first place.
- Demonstrate to those you meet that you have character and competence.

Enjoy

This is not serious business. Project upbeat feelings to everyone you meet. Reach out to others. Ask questions to get them talking about themselves and their agendas.

Meet Key Individuals

If people attending the event are wearing name tags, your job is easy. If they're not, ask someone you already know to direct or introduce you to others as you circulate. The event's organizers can be helpful, but approach them casually and don't ask too much at once or bother them when they're trying to orchestrate the next part of the program. The thing to remember is that you came to this event with a certain objective so you need to make a good effort to achieve it.

Demonstrate Character and Competence

Since this is a social occasion, all you have to do is make a pleasant first impression. You can show your positive qualities to good advantage in the way you handle meeting people you don't know. Appearing relaxed, warm, friendly, open, and straightforward gives others a sense of your character. Asking interesting, fun-to-answer questions that engage the other person and discreetly reveal things about yourself helps to paint a picture of your competence.

THE SCRIPT

As you circulate, ask good questions that start people talking about themselves and things that are important to them. Make mental notes of their answers so that you can write them down and review them after the event. Keep in mind that your purpose in collecting information is to determine the networking value of people you meet at the function.

If you're one of the many people who really feel uncomfortable making small talk, maybe this diagram of a conversational flow will help.

Let's go through a sample conversation to see how to link the components together, examining your side of the dialogue. (Of course, you would use your own conversational style and language.) This discussion should only take about five to 10 minutes.

Preliminaries: "Hi. My name's Dave Rosario." (Response) "Great party, isn't it?"

CONVERSATIONAL FLOW

Preliminaries
↓
Conversation Bridge
↓
Information Gathering
↓
Next Steps
↓
Conclusion

Making Conversation

Where is your industry going?

How is your company providing leadership?

How do you think your job is going to change as the industry adjusts itself?

Do you ever get the chance to speak on your company's or the industry's behalf?

Are you active in any industry associations?

Conversation Bridge: "I was on the planning committee last year. They asked me to help out this year, but things got so crazy at work I just couldn't give it enough time. I'm the production manager at Acme Building Supplies and we're getting our new line ready. What do you do, (name)?" (Response)

Information Gathering: Link the person's response to what you know, or would like to know, about his or her industry (see box for sample questions). You're trying to determine how the person is connected to his or her company's activities, the industry, and outside the industry. Is he or she a leader or role model for others and therefore a good networking connection? Lead to the next question by revealing something about you and your industry. Remember to be brief—you want the other person to do most of the talking.

Conversation Bridge (if you want to encourage a networking meeting): "It sounds like you've got some big challenges ahead of you. You know, from what you've been saying, it seems that we've got a lot of the same kinds of ideas." (Response)

Next Steps: "Why don't we get together for lunch sometime to see if we could give each other some support. What do you think?" (Response)

Conclusion: "Great. I'll give you a call next week." (On the other hand, if you decide you don't want to pursue a relationship with the person you're talking to, you can conclude like this: "I certainly enjoyed meeting you. It sounds like you've got some big challenges ahead of you. Good luck!")

When you network a room this way, you can have interesting, fun, and productive conversations with about four to eight people who could be potential networking partners. If one of these turns out to be a good connection for you, then your social savvy has paid off. Congratulations!

DOS AND DON'TS

Do: Prepare for social networking encounters.

Do: Assess the networking value of an event.

Do: Make sure you meet the people you came to meet.

Do: Impress those you meet with your character and competence.

Do: Ask targeted questions to help you evaluate a person's potential as a networking partner.

Don't: Attend an event with a vague idea that maybe you'll meet someone—with that mindset, you probably won't.

Don't: Go to every function you're invited to, or you won't have time for anything else.

Don't: Forget to have a good time!

In the Neighborhood: Networking on the Block

Many people miss a lot of networking opportunities because they mistakenly believe that networking stops when you leave the office and take off your business clothes. When it comes to making useful, informal networking connections, you need look no further than your backyard or front stoop. From block associations and town meetings to local volunteer clubs and spring cleanups, your neighborhood offers a multitude of networking possibilities for you.

The same concepts and creativity that apply to networking in your professional milieu also hold true for networking in your neighborhood. For example, one of your networking goals is to come into contact with many more people than you could possibly know by yourself. Look at what a gold mine your neighborhood turns out to be. Let's say that each of your neighbors has 25 social and work acquaintances who might someday be in a position to help you. This means that in a four-block-square neighborhood of about 50 homes, with two contacts per home, you have an untapped network of 2,500 people. In large cities, it's not unusual to find apartment buildings with 200 tenants, which gives networkers living there a universe of *5,000* possible contacts!

Of course, you wouldn't want to tap into more than a small fraction of that number. But you'll never have access to any of these contacts if you don't know your neighbors. And if you're just starting to get going with your networking plan, neighborhood networking can give you some valuable practice in a low-key, nonthreatening environment.

So let's expand our definition of networking to include *neighborhood networking*: enlarging your social environment and influence by developing and continuously nurturing relationships with neighbors and friends for mutual benefit.

In the 'Hood

Get to know your neighbors.
Join a neighborhood association.
Expand your territory to include the larger community.

GET TO KNOW YOUR NEIGHBORS

A lot of people are so tense and exhausted after a day at work that they just want to come home at night and crash. The most energy they want to expend is hitting the buttons on the TV remote control. It's a natural tendency to treat your home environment as a refuge from the workday world and to keep relationships with your neighbors superficial, confined to polite, noncommittal conversations and casual waves as you pass by. But I've found that active involvement in my neighborhood is so rewarding—and so much an extension of my business-oriented networking behavior—that it extends my concept of networking as a fun, engaging, and rewarding social experience.

My family and I moved to a quiet New Jersey suburb 14 years ago. Shortly after the last box was delivered, our next-door neighbors stopped by to welcome us. They described a neighborhood full of active, eclectic people who viewed neighbors as being just as important in their lives as their professional and business associates. Group activities ranged from monthly progressive dinners and block parties to hiking weekends and fishing trips. It was such an inviting environment that we couldn't resist—our entire family jumped in and took part in neighborhood goings-on.

I will admit that when it comes to getting results, networking among my neighbors doesn't have the same kind of payoff as my business networking. But it does open up new avenues for interaction with entities like the school board and local volunteer organizations. So I believe that being active in your neighborhood can be valuable for any networker because it expands your view of the world and helps you gain perspective on what's important to you.

JOIN A NEIGHBORHOOD ASSOCIATION

Whether you live in a city, suburb, or rural area, there are any number of neighborhood, community, or regional civic and recreational associations you can become a part of. Some are community watchdog groups that make sure that residents are represented fairly before town councils, planning boards, and other municipal bodies, while others concentrate on keeping the neighborhood clean or providing community services of some kind. Often, these organizations have a strong need for the same kinds of skills you bring to your workday role: good organization, creativity, resourcefulness, congeniality, a team spirit, focus, a sense of commitment, and a sincere desire to be useful. Working with one or more of these local groups not only gives you a chance to contribute to the well-being of your neighborhood but also introduces you to a wide spectrum of people from all walks of life.

If these groups have any downside, it's that they sometimes forget to have fun—the kind of fun that makes belonging to the organization, and working hard for it, all worthwhile. If the association you're interested in falls somewhat short in the fun category, you can help it to lighten up. Not only will this make it more enjoyable for you to take part but it can also rejuvenate the organization. When a group makes it more fun for people to be involved, it's not uncommon for membership to increase and for uninvolved members to start participating.

For example, you could spearhead an effort to match activities to members' needs by developing and distributing a questionnaire to find out what people's interests and priorities are, what types of events they'd like to sponsor, and how they'd like to participate in organizing activities. Based on the responses, help form committees to plan and implement each event, encouraging the groups to continue working together to build leadership, interest, and momentum.

You should find that involving yourself in your neighborhood in this way is a refreshing and useful shift from your business networking activity. And you'll be making social contacts that can provide a surprising boost to your networking activities when you least expect it.

EXPAND YOUR TERRITORY TO INCLUDE THE LARGER COMMUNITY

If you find neighborhood networking satisfying once you give it a try, don't overlook a larger neighborhood—your community—as equally fertile ground for networking. Participating on the community level can open up even more opportunities for you to help others as you help yourself. Applying the same principles to community groups as you would to your efforts with neighborhood associations should yield positive results.

Participating in Your Community

- City or town civic organizations
- Spruce-up campaigns
- Teen centers
- Youth groups such as Boy Scouts/Girl Scouts, Little League, and Big Brother/Big Sister
- Church, temple, or other religious organizations
- Groups that help the needy, such as food banks, soup kitchens, and homeless shelters
- Political clubs
- Social clubs
- Sports teams
- Cultural activities, such as local theater groups
- Museums and historical societies
- Garden clubs
- Chamber of Commerce
- Elks, Lions, and Rotary Clubs
- League of Women Voters
- Toastmasters

Let's take a look at a few of these activities to examine their networking potential. Say that the religious organization you belong to needs to upgrade its facilities. This effort will require the participation of congregants who have expertise in fund-raising, space planning, engineering, use variances, dealing with banks and local planning boards, environmental impact studies, safety standards reviews, financial planning, and public relations. What a host of different professionals you'd meet by taking part in this project!

Working with local youth groups would put you in contact with educators, school board members, teachers, police officers, social workers, politicians, and local business owners. How about coaching or playing on a local sports team? It wouldn't be unusual for you to strike up a friendship with your baseball team's second baseman (a firefighter) who introduces you to his neighbor, a corporate law firm partner, who knows a board member at the local bank, which has an interest in financing the shopping center project your construction company is bidding on. And if your team takes part in regional competitions, you expand your networking possibilities that much further.

A neighbor of mine has built up a lot of political capital over the years by taking political candidates around the area and introducing them to residents. Wanna-be town council representatives, mayors, school board members, and county agents consider a neighborhood tour with Bob an important part of their campaign. Bob doesn't have any political ambitions for himself. He's simply looking for good government and makes an effort to support candidates who he thinks will deliver it. In the process, though, he has gained influence—when he speaks out before the town council or school board on issues of community concern, the politicians he helped elect have been responsive to him.

You also want to keep your eyes open for special circumstances that could allow you to make a contribution to your community as well as enlarge your networking sphere. Here's an example. My brother and his wife own a communications design firm in San Francisco, a market where continuous networking is critical to being accepted in the business and social community. He heard that the San Francisco Bay Area Red Cross needed volunteer professionals to staff media communications posts activated when disaster relief efforts swing into action. This project brought together all types of Bay Area professionals representing a potpourri of organizations ranging from the Mayor's Office, the University of California, and the Legal Aid Society to Levi Strauss, Wells Fargo, and Pacific Bell. By participating, my brother provided a valuable community service while working shoulder-to-shoulder with top Bay Area communications specialists in a way that naturally broadened his connections in the community.

If you're so inclined and have the time, many community organizations are sorely in need of dynamic leadership—as you've probably realized by now, it's much easier to find workers than good leaders. But remember to choose carefully. Once you accept the mantle of leadership, it's sometimes hard to pass the baton to others. Unless there's a clear leadership succession plan for the organization, you easily can get stuck in the role.

There's an obvious, but often overlooked, caveat regarding neighborhood networking: don't get overextended. Networking in your immediate neighborhood or in the larger community can be so much fun that it's easy to let these activities cut into your valuable leisure time. The result is networking burnout, which can leave you so exhausted that you drop out of your extracurricular activities. To guard against this, be conservative in estimating how many commitments you can make and how much time you can devote to worthwhile activities. Remember that effective networking means long-term involvement, so pace yourself to make sure you have energy to devote to each of your many endeavors.

DOS AND DON'TS

Do: Use neighborhood networking as a way to develop your style in a low-key environment.

Do: Cultivate your neighbors both as friends and as potential networking partners.

Do: Consider your community an extension of your neighborhood for networking activities.

Don't: Think that networking stops when you get home.

Don't: Expect neighborhood networking to have the same kind of payoff as business networking.

Don't: Get overextended by making too many neighborhood and community commitments.

Expanding Your Horizons: Where to Go from Here

Well, you've done it. By now, you're an accomplished and successful one-to-one networker. Your presence reaches deeply into the community on a number of levels. It's gratifying to know and be known by movers and shakers in your business, social, and political environments.

At this point in your evolution as the consummate networker, you probably don't need more practice in developing your skills. But perhaps you could benefit from applying those skills somewhat differently. Many successful networkers find that once they know how to network effortlessly for professional and personal gain, they derive great satisfaction from networking for the "greater good" by getting involved in professional, social, and political causes that are important to them. Try these networking challenges on for size!

Organize Industry Roundtables

It doesn't take long for a well-positioned roundtable to become a dominant force in the business community. I've seen roundtables grow from a broad-based lunchtime discussion among a handful of executives to a well-organized program with concurrent sessions attracting hundreds of participants. The reason for the success of

141

New Challenges

- Organize industry roundtables that are important to the business community.
- Promote your favorite social cause with the help of a hand-picked task force.
- Encourage public sector reform and change in your community.

---

industry roundtables today rests with the current pace of business, which would be considered warp speed for the businessperson of 10 years ago. Many managers have to concentrate on short-term results and feel that long-range planning is a luxury they can't afford. A well-planned and well-staffed roundtable of experts (which, of course, would draw on the knowledge and experience of some of your networking partners) can inform and enlighten information-hungry businesspeople who are looking for fresh ideas and new ways to enhance their businesses.

I believe there's a very real need for exciting roundtables that will wake up and shake up participants. Many businesspeople have to depend on programs sponsored by trade associations to learn more about business issues that affect their future actions. The problem with these association programs is that too often they reflect the all too familiar middle-of-the-road thinking espoused by most of the organization's members. I'm suggesting an alternative: carefully designed programs that encourage long-range thinking and challenge participants to discuss and consider "what if" approaches as a foundation for industry change and development. As a skilled networker, you have a significant opportunity to strategically position a program to reach your target group. Use your networking connections to assemble a diverse and dynamic panel of speakers—including appropriate networking partners—who will stimulate and motivate participants to look at, and move in, new directions. Then stand back and see what happens.

I know a Midwestern commercial real estate pro who put together a very select roundtable of financial experts, site specialists, developers, packagers, and management experts. What started out as an intimate forum to discuss key events facing a local community's real estate market turned into an annual statewide happening attended by a hundred or so people who came to be seen, make contacts, do deals, influence the movers and shakers, and listen to what's happening in this volatile marketplace. It just goes to show that a good idea, effectively implemented, is a surefire winner that takes on a life of its own. Everyone will want to be a part of the success of such a roundtable approach and have an opportunity to add to the synergy of this exciting business forum.

Taking this kind of approach not only lets you use your networking partners' talents creatively but also greatly expands your networking connections as you interact with the many new and familiar friends taking part in your successful program. Awareness of your networking abilities, creativity, and business, leadership, and organizational skills can reach new heights when you plan and develop a project of this nature. For the seasoned networker, this can be the key that opens the door to years of exciting, productive networking encounters.

PROMOTE YOUR FAVORITE SOCIAL CAUSE

For some seasoned networkers, taking responsibility for an important social issue is just the challenge they're aching for. Recently, a handful of men and women from the Unitarian Society of Ridgewood, New Jersey, joined in an effort to provide self-sufficient senior citizens with affordable housing in a collegial, family-oriented environment—a situation that simply didn't exist in the state. After much planning, networking in the community, and meeting local, county, and state tests for communal housing, the group opened a residence that now houses 14 people. Since the Ridgewood experiment in senior living was started, about a half dozen other communities across the country have rallied to support similar projects.

There are so many pressing social needs in every community across America today that networkers of every inclination can easily find a worthwhile project to devote themselves to. If you live in a big city, for instance, you could marshal your network to help alleviate the problems of the hungry and homeless. Residents of an ecologically threatened area might want to join forces to save their environment. And networkers in any community would provide a great service by championing the needs of children. Whatever social cause you choose to commit your time and talents to, you can make a big difference by applying your substantial networking skills to a related project.

ENCOURAGE PUBLIC SECTOR REFORM

"School Budget Fails Again."

"Municipal Services Collapse Under Power Struggle."

"Town Rebuffs Troubled Teens."

Every day, in every community across the country, TV and newspaper headlines trumpet issues that cry out for reform and change. Sometimes, however, politicians are ill-equipped to bring about change because the solution requires business, organizational, and financial skills that outstrip available resources. Elected officials who truly want to reform the current system may be hampered by a lack of experience and funds to get the job done.

This is a perfect opportunity for the seasoned networker who cares deeply about the public welfare to get involved and make a measurable difference. When a change of administration takes place in your community, pick your target and jump in. The new mayor or council members might eagerly accept your offer of help.

A good example of how this approach works concerns how the mayor of Indianapolis, Indiana, drew on the resources of his community to focus on bringing down the high cost of providing citizens and the business community with essential services. Two years ago, Mayor Stephen Goldsmith was determined to fulfill a campaign pledge to reduce the size of city government. He set up a blue-ribbon panel of movers and shakers, including local business leaders, to spearhead task forces to review the city budget, find ways to improve performance of city employees, and reduce costs. One of the recommendations was to consider contracting out certain city services, allowing bids from city employees as well as outside contractors. This policy has already saved the city $18.5 million—and they're still working on it. As a result, Indianapolis is being perceived as a more desirable business location with lower business and personal taxes.

Whether you apply your networking skills to business, social, or political projects, whether you choose to create a program yourself or participate in an ongoing effort, you can make a major contribution to enhancing the quality of life in your community. In addition to the satisfaction you'll feel in making a difference, you can reap yet another benefit from these efforts: meeting other vital, active, and committed professionals like yourself to expand your network even further.

Who knows? Perhaps our paths will cross one day.

DOS AND DON'TS

Do: Find ways to use your networking acumen to "give back" to your community.

Do: Draw on the expertise of your networking partners to organize challenging business roundtables.

Do: Commit your networking skills and energies to a worthy social cause.

Do: Volunteer to help elected officials bring about civic reform.

Don't: Stop looking for networking challenges.

Don't: Hesitate to flex your networking muscles to get your partners involved in projects that are important to you.

Appendix: Sources for Making Contacts and Connections

Public libraries are a great source of information resources on networking opportunities. One very comprehensive reference book that is especially good for developing useful contacts is the *Encyclopedia of Associations*, published by Gale Research Company, in Detroit, now in its twenty-eighth edition.

This multivolume work lists information about nearly 23,000 national and international organizations, including trade, business, and commercial; environmental and agricultural; legal, governmental, public administration, and military; engineering, technological, and natural and social sciences; education; cultural; social welfare; health and medical; public affairs; fraternal, foreign interest, nationality, and ethnic; religious; veterans; hereditary, and patriotic; hobby and avocational; athletic and sports; labor unions, associations, and federations; chambers of commerce and trade and tourism; Greek-letter and related organizations; and fan clubs.

The following is an eclectic selection of entries that I hope will stimulate your imagination (reprinted with Gale's permission). Many associations welcome members from outside their industry.

Advertising Club of New York
235 Park Ave. South, 6th Floor
New York, NY 10003
Madhu Malhan, Director
(212) 533-8080
Founded: 1906
Members: 1,800

Professionals in advertising, publishing, marketing, and business. Sponsors educational and public service activities, promotional and public relations projects, and talks by celebrities and advertising persons. Conducts an annual advertising and marketing course, which offers classes in copy writing, special graphics, verbal communication, advertising production, sales promotion, marketing and management. Publications: *ACNY Membership Roster*, annual. ACNY Newsletter, quarterly.

Aerospace Education Foundation
1501 Lee Highway
Arlington, VA 22209-1198
Stephen S. Lee, Director
(703) 247-5839
Founded: 1956
Members: 2,000

Works to enhance public understanding of aerospace development; disseminate information concerning new accomplishments in fields of aerospace development and aerospace education; encourage students to pursue higher education in scientific, mathematical, and technological fields. Publication: *Newsletter*, quarterly. *Foundation Forums*, semiannual.

American Association for Artificial Intelligence
445 Burgess Dr.
Menlo Park, CA 94025
Carol M. Hamilton, Managing Director
(415) 328-3123
Founded: 1979
Members: 13,000
Artificial intelligence researchers, students, libraries, corporations, and others interested in the subject. (Artificial intelligence is a discipline in which an attempt is made to approximate the human thinking process through computers.) Areas of interest include interpretation of visual data, robotics, expert systems, natural language processing, knowledge representation, and artificial intelligence programming technologies. Publications: *AI Magazine*, quarterly. Includes association news, book reviews, employment opportunities, new products, and schedule of meetings and conferences.

American Electronics Association
5201 Great America Pkwy., Suite 520
Santa Clara, CA 95054
J. Richard Iverson, President
(408) 987-4200
Founded: 1943
Members: 3,500
Regional Groups: 23
Field Offices: 15
Trade association representing the U.S. electronics industry. Fosters a healthy business climate; conducts networking programs for industry executives. Committees: Customs; Domestic Public Affairs; Education and Science Legislative; Education and Science Policy; EOH Export Controls; Government Business; Government Relations. Publications: *American Electronics Association Directory*, annual. *Membership Directory*. *American Electronics Associa-*

tion Update, monthly. Association and trade news publication; includes legislative briefs, electronics and information technology industry statistics and calendar of events.

American Society of Concrete Construction
1902 Techny Ct.
Northbrook, IL 60062
W. Burr Bennett Jr., Executive Vice President
(312) 291-0270
Founded: 1964
Members: 900

General contractors and subcontractors working with concrete; allied businesses, such as ready-mix producers, equipment manufacturers, and other suppliers and distributors. Seeks to stimulate professional responsibility and reliability; encourage the research and development of concrete; facilitate technical and practical education. Publications: *ASCC Management Report,* periodic. *ASCC Membership Bulletin*, periodic. *ASCC Membership Directory*, annual.

Association of Biotechnology Companies
1666 Connecticut Ave., NW, Suite 330
Washington, DC 20009-1039
William E. Small, Executive Director
Founded: 1983
Members: 320
Regional Groups: 9
Local Groups: 3

Provides information on biotechnology issues pertaining to U.S. and international regulations, patents, finance, and other problems confronting members. Organizes workshops and seminars; maintains education dialogue with Congress, non-U.S. government bodies, regulatory agencies, and the public. Publications: *ABC Alerts*, periodic. *Details*, newsletter focusing on federal regulatory and legislative developments affecting the biotechnology industry.

Associated General Contractors of America
1957 E St., NW
Washington, DC 20006
Hubert Beatty, Executive Vice President
(201) 393-2040
Founded: 1918
Members: 32,500
Local Groups: 101

General construction contractors; subcontractors; industry suppliers; service firms. Provides market services through its divisions. Conducts special conferences and seminars designed specifically for construction firms. Maintains 65 committees. Publications: *AGC Membership Directory and Buyer's Guide*, annual. *Constructor*, monthly. Also publishes manual, guides, model contract documents, studies, and checklists.

Association of Management Analysts in State and Local
  Government
University of Pennsylvania
3814 Walnut St.
Philadelphia, PA 19104
Dr. Thomas Mills, Secretary-Treasurer
(215) 898-8212
Founded: 1963
Members: 320

Management analysts from business and state and local government, professors, and heads of university and public service institutes and state training institutes facilitate interchange of information in the field of management analysis. Publications: *Conference Papers*, annual. *Directory of Members and Conference Attendees*, annual. *MASLIG Messenger*, quarterly. Newsletter reporting on projects in the field of management analysis. Contains membership profiles.

Credit Research Foundation
8815 Center Park Dr.
Columbia, MD 21045
R. F. Thompson, President
(410) 740-5499
Founded: 1949
Members: 500

Credit, financial, and working capital executives of manufacturing and banking concerns. Objective is to create a better understanding of the impact of credit on the economy. Plans, supervises, and administers research and educational programs. Conducts surveys on economic conditions, trends, policies, practices, theory, systems, and methodology. Sponsors formal educational programs in credit and financial management. Publications: *Compensation of Credit Executives*, biennial. *CRF Publications Summary*, periodic. *Monthly Staff Report*. Covers technical topics in the field of credit management. *National Summary of Domestic Trade Receivables*, quarterly. Newsletter provides benchmarks on the basis of which credit executives may develop forecasts, compare the general condition of their trade receivables, and evaluate the effectiveness of their collection operations with the standard for the industry.

Eastern Finance Association
Georgia Southern University
Department of Finance
PO Box 8151
Statesboro, GA 30460
Dr. Lon M. Carnes, Executive Director
(912) 681-5437
Founded: 1965
Members: 1,900

College and university professors and financial officers; corporations, banks, and nonprofit organizations. Provides a meeting place for persons interested in any aspect of finance, including financial management, investments, and banking. Publications: *Financial Review*, quarterly.

Financial Executives Institute
10 Madison Ave.
PO Box 1938
Morristown, NJ 07962-1938
P. Norman Roy, President
(201) 898-4600
Founded: 1931
Members: 13,505
Local Groups: 91

Professional organization of corporate financial executives performing duties of controller, treasurer, or vice president, finance. Sponsors research activities through its affiliated Financial Executives Research Foundation. Committees: Academic Relations; Corporate Finance; Corporate Reporting; Employee Benefits; Government Business; Government Liaison. Publications: *FEI Briefings*, monthly. *Financial Executive*, bimonthly. Magazine for senior financial officers in large and mid-sized firms. Examines the latest developments in business, government, and economics from the perspective of the financial executive.

Graphic Communications Association
100 Daingerfield Rd.
Alexandria, VA 22314
Norman W. Scharpf, President
(703) 519-8160
Founded: 1966
Members: 350

A national affiliate of Printing Industries of America. Printers, publishers, advertising agencies, separation houses, and manufacturers provide for exchange of information and experience related to graphic arts print production. Conducts tutorial programs, seminars, workshops, systems research, and conferences. Publications: *Membership Directory*, annual. *GCA Review*, monthly. Newsletter providing information on current activities and new developments.

Information Technology Association of America
1616 North Fort Meyer Dr., Suite 1300
Arlington, VA 22209
Luanne James, Executive Director
(703) 522-5055
Founded: 1960
Members: 700

Companies offering computer software and services to the public. Seeks to improve management methods, develop service possibilities, and define standards of performance. Conducts conferences and seminars; provides public and governmental relations programs. Other program areas include: competitive practices; data communications; education and small business interests; image; research and statistics. Maintains speakers bureau and charitable programs. Committees: Education and Information Services; Government Relations; Image/Public Communications; Research and Statistics. Publications: *ITAA Membership Directory*, annual. *Contracts Reference Directory*, periodic. *DATA Newsletter*, bimonthly. *Salary Study*, annual. *Survey of State Taxation*, quarterly. *Technical Information Services*, periodic.

International Association of Printing House Craftsmen
7042 Brooklyn Blvd.
Minneapolis, MN 55429-1370
Kevin Keane, Executive Director
(612) 560-1620
Founded: 1919
Members: 12,000
Local Groups: 118

Owners, superintendents, foremen, and assistant foremen of printing plants; associate members are manufacturers' representatives and industry suppliers. Conducts field trips and workshops; maintains speakers bureau; sponsors education programs. Sponsors International Printing Week and competitions; bestows awards from Gallery of Superb Printing. Publications: *Craftsmen Communicator*, bimonthly. *Craftsmen Review*, quarterly. Covers the events and activities of the various clubs of the associations. Includes directory of clubs.

National Association of Chemical Distributors
1101 17th Street NW, Suite 1200
Washington, DC 20036
Joseph A. Cook, Executive Vice President
(202) 296-9200
Founded: 1971
Members: 265
Regional Groups: 5
Firms that purchase, store, and transport industrial chemicals. To enhance and promote the professionalism of the industry; to promote safe practices, educate managers, exchange ideas, and inform other sectors of the chemical industry of the role of distributors. Committees: Canadian Liaison; Chemicals Distribution Advancement. Publications: *Action Bulletin*, periodic. *Chemical Distributor Newsletter*. *Government Affairs Update*, periodic. *Membership Roster*, annual.

National Association of Towns and Townships
1522 K Street, NW, Suite 600
Washington, DC 20005
Jeffrey H. Schiff, Executive Director
(202) 737-5200
Founded: 1963
Members 13,000

Federation of state organizations and individual communities. Provides technical assistance, education services, and public policy support to local government offices of small communities across the country. Conducts research and develops public policy recommendations to help improve the quality of life for people living in small communities. Sponsors educational conferences and training workshops. Bestows Grassroots Government Leadership Award and Legislator of the Year Award. Publication: *NaTaT's Reporter*, monthly. Tabloid covering small town and rural government.

National Civic League
1445 Market, Suite 300
Denver, CO 80202-1728
John Parr, President
(305) 571-4343
Founded: 1894
Members: 2,000

Government leaders, educators, public officials, civic organization, libraries, and businesses interested in improving state and local government and developing techniques of citizen action. Serves as a clearinghouse for information on state constitutions, city and county charters, state and local government organization, legislative apportionment, election systems, fiscal procedures, ethics and campaign finance, and techniques of citizen participation. Sponsors All-America City Awards. Publications: *Annual Report. National Civic Review: Building Successful Communities*, bimonthly. Journal on community problem-solving, including information on technology transfer, government management and productivity, performance measurement, public finance, and community trends. Contains annual index, calendar of events, and case studies.

National Management Association
2210 Arbor Blvd.
Dayton, Ohio 45439
Ronald E. Leigh, President
(513) 294-0421
Founded: 1925
Members: 74,000
Regional Groups: 6
Local Groups: 255

Business and industrial management personnel; membership comes from supervisory level, with the remainder from middle management and above. Seeks to develop and recognize management as a profession and to promote the free enterprise system. Presents Executive of the Year Award at annual conventions; maintains speakers bureau. Committees: Free Enterprise; Industry/ Government Activities; Management Certification; Management Development; Productivity. Publications: *Board of Directors Directory*, annual. *Manage*, quarterly. *National Speakers' Directory*, periodic.

National Soft Drink Association
1101 16th Street NW
Washington, DC 20036
William L. Ball III, President
(202) 463-6732
Founded: 1919
Members: 1,700
State Groups: 47

Active members are manufacturers of soft drinks; associate members are suppliers of materials and services. Objectives include government affairs—activities on the national and state levels; discussion of industry problems; general improvements of operating procedures. Committees: Federal Affairs; Membership; Scientific and Regulatory Affairs; State and Environmental Affairs. Publications: *Membership Directory and Buyer's Guide*, annual. *NSDA News*, monthly. Covers legislative issues affecting soft drink bottlers and suppliers to the soft drink industry.

The Planning Forum
PO Box 70
Oxford, OH 45056
Tom Quilter, President
(513) 523-4185
Founded: 1985
Members: 6,500
Local Groups: 44

Professional society primarily comprised of executives involved in international strategic management and planning. Presents awards; conducts seminars; provides placement services. Conducts research and education programs; sponsors competitions. Publications: *Membership Directory*, annual. *Network*, monthly. Newsletter containing book and media summaries and strategic management articles. *Planning Review*, bimonthly. Journal includes case studies, reports, and literature search.

Product Development and Management Association
Indiana University
Graduate School of Business
801 West Michigan Ave.
Indianapolis, IN 46202-5151
Thomas P. Hustad, Secretary-Treasurer
(800) 232-5241
Founded: 1976
Members: 1,050
Local Groups: 5

Managers working in product innovation, teachers and researchers in the area of product innovation management, product planning and development process; product innovation consultants; market research firms; new product institutes; advertising agencies and media; testing companies; trade associations. Promotes improved product innovation management by drawing upon members' resources. Encourages research designed to make product innovation management more effective and efficient; provides forum for the exchange of ideas and findings among universities, industry, government, and related sectors. Bestows Innovator of the Year Award. Publications: *Journal of Product Innovation Management*, quarterly. Presents research, experiences and insights of academics, etc. *PDMA Membership Directory* includes companies and geographic index.

Production and Operations Management Society
University of Baltimore
1420 North Charles St.
Baltimore, MD 21202
Kalyan Singhai, President
(410) 625-3307
Founded: 1989
Members: 1,000

Production and operations management professionals and academics. Works to advance POM technology and practice. Provides a forum for interaction between business and engineering schools, corporations and government. Sponsors practitioners, workshops, conferences, and seminars. Encourages the development of production and operation curriculums. Bestows awards for best dissertation, best paper by students and recent graduates, the Abernathy Award for best paper in management of technology, and Orlicky Award for best innovation in manufacturing services. Publications: *POM Spectrum*, quarterly. *Newsletter. Production and Operations Management*, quarterly.

React International
PO Box 998
Wichita, KS 67201
Deanne Earwood, Office Manager
(316) 263-2100
Founded: 1962
Members: 10,000
Local groups: 700

A public service communications organization supported by commercial, governmental, and private membership funds. Provides volunteer public service and emergency communications through citizens band two-way radios. Assists in all local emergencies by furnishing instant radio communication in cooperation with proper authorities. Sponsors competitions, maintains speakers bureau; bestows awards; compiles statistics. Publication: *Newsletter*, bimonthly. *React Team Director*, annual.

Special Interest Group for Business Data Processing and
    Management
c/o Association for Computing Machinery
1515 Broadway, 17th Floor
New York, NY 10036
Elias Awad, Chairman
(212) 869-7440
Founded: 1960
Members: 4,625

A special interest group of the Association for Computing Machinery. Primary interest is in the use of computers in the business environment. Places emphasis on pragmatic business information systems that utilize advanced technology where beneficial. Areas of interest include: long-range planning for information systems; information systems cost/benefit analysis techniques; database/data communications approaches and selection. Publications: *Database*, quarterly.

Below are the name and address of over 500 Toastmaster Clubs, excerpted from an extensive listing provided by *Toastmasters International*. Each of the clubs listed has been active for a minimum of ten years. Club longevity is a credit to the value of the Toastmaster concept and the vitality of individual clubs throughout the U.S. If a convenient location for you is not listed, the headquarters can usually locate a club nearby. Call (714)-858-8255 for more information.

Arizona

Dobson Ranch
Ranch House Restaurant
2155 S Dobson Rd.
Ahwatukee, AZ
602-961-0935

Gilbert
Smitty's Restaurant
1951 N Alma School Rd.
Chandler, AZ
602-963-4760

Sunset
Little America
2515 E Butler
Flagstaff, AZ
602-526-9046

Daybreakers
Charter Hospital
6015 W Peoria Ave.
Glendale, AZ
602-934-2057

Grogan Green Valley
First Interstate Bank
375 W Continental Rd.
Green Valley, AZ
602-648-2650

Superstition
Shoneys Restaurant
1910 S Gilbert Rd.
Mesa, AZ
602-827-0790

Paradise Valley
The Forum Pueblo Norte
7090 E Mescal St. 2d Fl.
Paradise Valley, AZ
602-996-6070

Ocotillo
Lexington Hotel
100 W Clarendon St.
Phoenix, AZ
602-253-5832

Sunrise
The University Club
39 E Monte Vista
Phoenix, AZ
602-280-1000

Kachina
Bank Of America
101 N 1st. Ave.
Conference Room
Phoenix, AZ
602-978-1903

Camelback
Smitty's Restaurant
2727 W Bell Rd.
Phoenix, AZ
602-486-0463

Roundup
1st. United Meth. Church
5510 N Central Ave.
Phoenix, AZ
602-242-5634

Dawn Busters
Coco's Rest. Metro Center
2740 W North Lane
Phoenix, AZ
602-997-4244

Prescott
The Unity Church
145 S Arizona St.
Prescott, AZ
602-632-5724

Western Sages
Scottsdale Symphony Assn.
3817 Brown Ave.
Scottsdale, AZ
602-832-2903

Easy Risers
Scottsdale Senior Center
7375 E 2nd. St., Rm. 3
Scottsdale, AZ
602-988-3212

Tri City
Vista Del Camino Park
7700 E Roosevelt
Scottsdale, AZ
602-956-7528

Scottsdalians
Scottsdale Senior Center
7375 E Second St.
Scottsdale, AZ
602-947-9196

Oak Creek Orators
Sedona Adult Comm. Ctr.
2645 Melody Lane
Sedona, AZ
602-284-0179

Cochise
Landmark Cafe
400 W Fry Blvd.
Sierra Vista, AZ
602-458-5280

Speaking First
First Interstate Bank
711 West Broadway
Tempe, AZ
602-961-1067

Tempe
Smitty's Restaurant
3232 S Mill Ave.
Tempe, AZ
602-838-7706

Twilite
Pyle Adult Rec. Center
655 E Southern Ave.
Tempe, AZ
602-961-0531

University
Arizona State University
Memorial Union Rm. 211
Tempe, AZ
602-730-6208

Saguaro No. 16
Church of The Nazarene
404 S Columbus Ave.
Tucson, AZ
602-327-8998

Los Nortenos
Johnnie's Restaurant
4040 E 22nd. St.
Tucson, AZ
602-747-8687

U of A Granada
Armory Park Senior Ctr.
220 S 5th. Ave.
Tucson, AZ
602-326-8579

Roadrunners
Coco's Restaurant
6095 E Broadway
Tucson, AZ
602-299-8283

Sunrisers
Carrow's Restaurant
2660 N Campbell Ave.
Tucson, AZ
602-299-3014

California

Alameda
Alameda Historical High
   School
2200 Central Ave.
Alameda, CA
510-769-1886

Anaheim Breakfast
Carrow's Restaurant
100 N State College Ave.
Anaheim, CA
714-771-3600

Tri-City Achievers
Carrow's Restaurant
100 N State College Blvd.
Anaheim, CA
714-937-0880

Harbor Lites
Newport Beach Country Club
1600 E Pacific Coast
Balboa, CA
714-509-9436

Capital Speakers
Benicia Chamber of Commerce
601 1st. St.
Benicia, CA
707-745-9625

Berkeley Storymasters
Berkeley Downtown Library
Kittridge & Shattuck
Berkeley, CA
415-642-8190

Filibusters
McDonalds Community Room
825 Imperial Highway
Brea, CA
714-694-2086

Brea
Brea Library Meeting Room
1 Civic Center Circle
Brea, CA
714-970-5074

76 Speakers Forum
Unocal Research Center
376 S Valencia Avenue
Brea, CA
714-693-6816

Table Talkers
Plaza Inn Motel
7039 Orangethorpe Ave.
Buena Park, CA
714-522-6434

Knotts Speak Easy
Chicken Dinner Restaurant
Knotts Berry Farm
Buena Park, CA
310-598-1404

Valley Times
Bakers Square Restaurant
1461 W Campbell Ave.
Campbell, CA
408-264-2310

Switch-On
Coco's Restaurant
330 E Hamilton Ave.
Campbell, CA
408-261-1684

Castro Valley
Unity Church
20121 Santa Maria Ave.
Castro Valley, CA
510-538-8971

Los Cerritos
Coco's Restaurant
11510 E South St.
Cerritos, CA
310-867-3265

Eclectic Dialectics
Coco's Restaurant
11510 E South St.
Cerritos, CA
714-826-4544

Sun Valley
Baker's Square
1680 Willow Pass Rd.
Concord, CA
510-939-9197

Toastmasters Breakfast Club
Baker's Square
1680 Willow Pass Rd.
Concord, CA
510-848-3277

Newport Beach
Continental Insurance Building
3080 S Bristol St.
Costa Mesa, CA
714-759-5478

Blue Flame
Colombo's Cafe & Bakery
2610 S Harbor Blvd.
Costa Mesa, CA
714-786-5160

Costa Mesa
OC Dept. of Education
200 Kalmus Drive
Costa Mesa, CA
714-549-8211

Community Speak E-Z
Faith Community Church
15906 E San Bernardino
Covina, CA
818-337-9509

Covina Breakfast Club
Covina Bowl
1060 W San Bernardino
Covina, CA
818-969-8564

Cullver City
V M B Senior Center, Rm. 4
4150 Overland Ave.
Culver City, CA
213-939-6470

Cupertino
Carrow's Restaurant
10630 S De Anza Blvd.
Cupertino, CA
408-996-8676

Daly City Toastmasters
33 Gellert Office Building
Conference Room
33 Gellert
Daly City, CA
510-682-7093

Dana Harbor
Dana Harbor Group & Youth
  Facility
34451 Ensenada
Dana Point, CA
714-248-8299

Danville Toastmasters
P G & E Learning Center
2211 Camino Ramon
Danville, CA
510-462-6930

Downey Space
Sakvatore's Pasta House
12056 Paramont Blvd.
Downey, CA
310-803-5203

Downey Breakfast
Mimi's Cafe
8157 E Firestone Blvd.
Downey, CA

Rising Stars
Cafe N Stuff
9306 Firestone Blvd.
Downey, CA
310-790-8082

Earth Save
Neighborhood Comm. Ctr.
1845 Park Ave.
Fountain Valley, CA
714-963-1211

Surfside Speakers
F V Regional Hospital HRC
Trailer-17100 Euclid
Fountain Valley, CA
714-842-8241

F U N
Golden Bay Title #107
39111 Paseo Padre Pkwy.
Fremont, CA
510-656-1593

Pathfinder
Development Center
39550 Liberty St.
Fremont, CA
510-656-3738

Star Search
Golden Bay Title Ins.
39111 Paseo Padre Pkwy.
Fremont, CA
510-794-8958

Moving On
Coco's Coffee Shop
12582 Valley View
Garden Grove, CA
310-492-1237

Garden Grove Toasters
Fullerton Savings Bank
Euclid at Acacia Pkwy.
Garden Grove, CA
714-636-0998

Mensanity
Garden Grove Hospital
12601 Garden Grove Blvd.
Garden Grove, CA
714-645-7612

Valley Speakers
Hacienda Hts. Christian
   Church
15716 E Tetley
Hacienda Heights, CA
310-945-7787

San Gabriel Valley
Puente Hills Med. Ctr.
1850 S Azusa Ave.
Hacienda Heights, CA
818-810-5386

Skywest
Lyons Restaurant
25010 Hesperian Blvd.
Hayward, CA
510-785-4290

Spokesmen
Coco's Restaurant
6886 Bolsa Ave.
Huntington, CA
714-898-2826

Rise and Shiners
Coco's Restaurant
6886 Bolsa Ave.
Huntington Beach, CA
714-374-1240

Irvine Complex
Pepperdine University
2151 Michelson Dr., Rm. 9
Irvine, CA
714-552-1645

Saddleback Valley
United Way Bldg.
23421 S Pointe Dr.
Laguna Hills, CA
714-951-2978

Lake Forest
Polly's Pies Restaurant
23701 Moulton Pkwy
Laguna Hills, CA
714-859-7117

Real-Time Ambassadors
Clifton's Lakewood
77 Lakewood Center Mall
Lakewood, CA
310-432-9344

Tri-City
Tri-Valley Brokers
1988 4th St. At "L"
Livermore, CA
510-447-0103

Gavel
Coast Federal Bank
13900 Seal Beach Blvd.
Long Beach, CA
310-429-3939

Talk & Tell
L.B. Board of Realtors
3747 Long Beach Blvd.
Long Beach, CA
310-424-2239

Century City
Rancho PK Golf Course
10460 W Pico Blvd.
Los Angeles, CA
301-823-4477

S.O.M.
Hamburger Henry
Wilshire Blvd. & 30th
Los Angeles, CA
213-934-5451

Southern Marin
Shakeys Pizza
Strawberry Shopping Ctr.
Mill Valley, CA
415-383-0451

Saddleback Sunrise
Mission Viejo Country Club
26200 Country Club
Mission Viejo, CA
714-661-3699

Mission Viejo
Denny's Restaurant
24445 Alicia Pkwy.
Mission Viejo, CA
714-364-1644

Monterey Peninsula
Holiday Inn Resorts
1000 Aguajito Rd.
Monterey, CA
408-375-6236

Cypress
Church of Christ
176 Central Ave.
Monterey, CA
408-375-5525

Newark
Newark Library
6300 Civic Terrace Dr.
Newark, CA
510-796-3031

Newport Center
Pacific Mutual Ins. Co.
700 Newport Center Dr.
Newport Beach, CA
714-730-7117

Montebello
Montebello City Hall
1600 W Beverly Blvd.
Norwalk, CA
818-932-2509

Oakland 88
Prov. Hosp. Conf. A 3rd. F
S Wing 3100 Summit
Oakland, CA
510-452-0151

Merritt
Summit Medical Center
3100 Summit
Oakland, CA
510-834-8713

Oakland City Center
Clorox-13th Fl. Conf. Rm.
1221 Broadway Ave.
Oakland, CA
510-271-7575

Paul Revere
Coco's Restaurant
2585 N Tustin Ave.
Orange, CA
714-771-3600

Peddler's
Business Automation
1572 N Main St.
Orange, CA
714-998-6600

Orange Motivators
Evangelical Free Church
1350 E Taft Rm. 115
Orange, CA
714-997-1036

Pacifica P M
Pacifica Comm. Center
540 Crespi Dr.
Pacifica, CA
415-761-0216

Lee Emerson Bassett
School of Business
Stanford University
Palo Alto, CA
415-493-8023

Varian
Varian Assoc. Conf. Rm. C
3100 Hansen Way
Palo Alto, CA
415-424-6463

Early Risers
Lyon's Restaurant
4298 El Camino Real
Palo Alto, CA
415-493-7350

Petaluma
Hermann Sons Hall
Western & Webster
Petaluma, CA
707-778-8174

Diablo Champagne
Marie Callenders
22090 Diamond Blvd.
Pleasant Hill, CA
510-685-8095

Amador Valley
Carrows Restaurant
7505 Dublin Blvd.
Pleasanton, CA
510-351-6566

Peninsula
Raffaello Restorante
400 S Pacific Ave.
Rancho Palos Ver, CA
310-316-6573

Donald L. Bogie
First United Methodist Church
2915 Broadway
Redwood City, CA
415-363-8723

Richmond Breakfast
Richmond Comm.
   Development
330 - 25th St.
Richmond, CA
510-222-2510

Gold Brickers
John Steinbeck Library
110 W San Luis
Salinas, CA
408-739-7317

Salinas Sunrise
Lyon's Restaurant
1250 South Main St.
Salinas, CA
408-422-5960

Steinbeck
Steinbeck Library Meeting Rm.
110 W San Luis St.
Salinas, CA
408-424-2247

Golden Gate
The Mills Bldg. Rm. 1091
220 Montgomery St.
San Francisco, CA
415-983-4669

Crownmasters
Shaklee Bldg.
1144 Market St., 2nd. Fl.
San Francisco, CA
510-483-1296

Nugget Masters
Bank of California - CA RM
400 California St., 5th Fl.
San Francisco, CA
415-393-1600

Magic Word
Parkmerced Act Office
345 Vidal Dr.
San Francisco, CA
415-239-2708

Money Talks
Federal Reserve Bank/SF
101 Market St.
San Francisco, CA
415-974-2810

San Jose Toastmasters Club
Coco's Restaurant
330 E Hamilton Ave.
San Jose, CA
408-374-6571

North Valley
4th Street Bowl
1441 N 4th. St.
San Jose, CA
408-272-9555

Bayfair
Denny's Restaurant
15015 Freedom Ave.
San Leandro, CA
510-538-6025

San Leandro
San Leandro Public Library
300 Estudillo Ave.
San Leandro, CA
510-351-1293

San Mateo
San Mateo City Hall
320 W 20th. Ave.
San Mateo, CA
415-341-2681

Positive Thinking
Villa/Quality Hotel
4000 S El Camino Real
San Mateo, CA
415-871-5277

Marin
Celia's Mexican Restaurant
1 Vivian Way
San Rafael, CA
415-453-3034

Lucas Green
Fireman's Fund Ins.
1600 Los Gamos Dr.
San Rafael, CA
415-492-6040

Danville
Father Nature's Restaurant
172 East Prospect Ave.
San Ramon, CA
510-743-0933

Smedley Number One
Int'l House of Pancake
1001 W 17th St.
Santa Ana, CA
714-573-0542

Century
Pomona 1st Federal
17851 17th St.
Santa Ana, CA
714-544-3357

Liberty Singles
Village Farmer Restaurant
1651 Sunflower Ave.
Santa Ana, CA
714-499-5353

West Valley Orators
Denny's Restaurant
1745 El Camino Real
Santa Clara, CA
408-379-6402

Rolman Forum
"Rolm, A Siemers Company"
4900 Old Ironside Dr.
Santa Clara, CA
408-492-4065

Santa Cruz Downtown
Peachwoods
555 Highway 17
Santa Cruz, CA
408-724-3792

Surf City Speakers
Goodwill Industries
350 Encinal
Santa Cruz, CA
408-425-1663

Dynamic Forcemasters
S F S Public Library
11712 E Telegraph Rd.
Santa Fe Springs, CA
310-928-2658

Santa Monica
L. A. Fresh
11819 Wilshire Blvd.
Santa Monica, CA
310-471-1829

Toastmasters-By-The-Sea
Viva La Pasta
12121 Wilshire Blvd.
Santa Monica, CA
310-458-9382

Kaycee 638
La Fresh Restaurant
11819 Wilshire Blvd.
Santa Monica, CA
213-475-7713

Santa Rosa
The Villa Restaurant
3910 Montgomery Dr.
Santa Rosa, CA
707-573-8703

Saratoga Toastmasters
Westhope Presbyterian
12850 Saratoga Ave.
Saratoga, CA
408-241-6737

Wordmasters
Fidelity Federal Bank
13820 Seal Beach Blvd.
Seal Beach, CA
714-841-4127

Leisure World
Coast Federal Bank
13900-A Seal Beach Blvd.
Seal Beach, CA
310-433-5575

Sonoma
Westlake Wine Country House
800 Oregon St.
Sonoma, CA
707-996-4926

South Gate
Int'l House of Pancakes
4024 Tweedy Blvd.
South Gate, CA
714-476-3530

Communicators
South Pasadena Library
1100 Oxley St.
South Pasadena, CA
818-447-0505

Golden Years
Municipal Building
33 Arroyo Dr.
South San Francisco, CA
415-570-6971

Lumberyacks
Kemper Insurance
475 Sansome St., 5th. Fl.
South San Francisco, CA
415-616-6529

St. Helena
Boys & Girls Club of St.
    Helena
1255 Oak Ave.
St. Helena, CA
707-963-9034

Speak 4 Yourself
Samtrans Building
1250 San Carlos Blvd.
Sunnyvale, CA
408-735-5421

Habits
Lockheed Learning Center
1345 Moffett Park Dr.
Sunnyvale, CA
415-960-3639

Temple City
El Gordos Restaurant
960 E Las Tunas Dr.
Temple City, CA
818-571-6913

South Bay
Int'l House of Pancakes
21710 Hawthorne Blvd.
Torrance, CA
310-377-4149

Harbor Lights
Torrance West Annex
3031 Torrance Blvd.
Torrance, CA
310-830-6545

Bay Cities
West End Tennis Club
4343 Spencer St.
Torrance, CA
310-373-5556

Sensational Salesmen
Pomona 1st Federal S & L
17851 17th St.
Tustin, CA
714-669-2870

Tustin
Pomona First S & L
17th & Prospect
Tustin, CA
714-955-1991

Union City
Union City Library
34007 Alvarado-Niles
Union City, CA
510-785-9903

Mare Island
Kaiser Perm Hospital
975 Sereno Dr. 7th Fl.
Vallejo, CA
707-643-7361

Sunrise
Theatre Cafe
1655 N Main St.
Walnut Creek, CA
510-295-4412

Diablo
Copper Skillett
700 Bancroft Ave.
Walnut Creek, CA
510-932-6746

Pajaro Valley
Farmers Insurance
734 E Lake Ave., Suite 10
Watsonville, CA
408-728-2220

Westwinds
West Covina Comm. Center
2501 East Cortez
West Covina, CA
909-595-0840

Dynamic Whittier
Presbyterian Hospital
12401 Washington Blvd.
Whittier, CA
310-863-7088

Whittier
Presbyterian Hospital
12401 E Washington Blvd.
Whittier, CA
310-698-3140

District of Columbia

Kohoutex
Penn. Baptist Church
3000 Penn. Ave. SE
Washington, DC
202-581-0393

Capitol Hill
Longworth House Office
Building Rm. 1129
Indep & NJ Ave.
Washington, DC
202-225-4021

E P A
EPA Education Ctr. Breakroom
USEPA - 401 M St. SW
Washington, DC
202-260-5251

Speechmasters
FAA Bldg., 9 Fl. Meeting
  Room
800 Indep Ave. SW
Washington, DC
202-267-9094

F E M A
Fed. Emergency Mgt. Agency
500 C St. SW Rm. 401
Washington, DC
202-646-4171

OCC Speakeasies
Comptroller/Currency
250 E St. SW
Washington, DC
202-874-4755

Matthews Memorial
Matthews Mem. Baptist
    Church
2616 M.L.King Jr. Ave. SE
Washington, DC
301-474-9149

Florida

Foliage
Erroll Oaks Club House
1435 Oak Place B
Apopka, FL
407-880-9619

Boca Raton
Historical Train Depot
745 S Dixie Hwy.
Boca Raton, FL
407-394-7963

Bradenton
Bradenton Herald Bldg.
102 Manatee Ave. West
Bradenton, FL
813-778-6842

Clearwater
Robby's Pancake House
1617 Gulf-to-Bay Blvd.
Clearwater, FL
813-734-3792

Edward H. White
Dixie Restaurant
U.S. 1
Cocoa, FL
407-784-4789

Coral Gables
Sizzler Restaurant
11415 S Dixie Hwy.
Coral Gables, FL
305-264-9752

Miracle Mile
Howard Johnson Rest.
1430 South Dixie Hwy.
Coral Gables, FL
305-666-8067

Achievers
Target Store
6250 West Sample Rd.
Coral Springs, FL
407-750-4001

Davie
Arrowhead Country Club
Nova Dr.
Davie, FL
305-436-5809

Daytona Beach
ARC Building # 2
100 Jimmy Huger Circle
Daytona Beach, FL
904-274-5606

West Volusia
Watson Realty
1961 S Woodland Blvd.
De Land, FL
407-736-6402

Donoghue-Dunedin
Countryside High School
3000 SR 580 Rm. A-3
Dunedin, FL
813-734-2023

Venetian
Denny's Restaurant
3151 NW 9th Ave.
Fort Lauderdale, FL
305-565-8608

Great Fort Lauderdale
Shoney's Restaurant
1431 N Federal Hwy.
Fort Lauderdale, FL
305-760-4510

Ft. Myers
Smitty's Restaurant
2240 W 1st St.
Fort Myers, FL
813-540-0055

Friendly
Cleveland Clinic Hospital
2835 N Ocean Blvd.
Ft. Lauderdale, FL
305-968-6563

Gainesville
Barnett Bank
1961 N Main St.
Gainesville, FL
904-372-8666

Gainesville Sunrise
CH2M Hill
7201 NW 11th Place
Gainesville, FL
904-375-2248

Eddie Rickenbacker
Florida PWR & Light Cafeteria
Rm. 2150 W 68th St.
Hialeah, FL
305-821-2345

Good Morning
Resource Center
1903 Hollywood Blvd.
Hollywood, FL
305-476-8066

Southside
Southside Assembly/God
Flshp Hall-1842 Olevia
Jacksonville, FL
904-399-1077

Arlington
Int'l House of Pancakes
5221 University Blvd. W
Jacksonville, FL
904-725-1665

Top O The Rock
Prudential Ins. Cafe
701 San Marco Blvd.
Jacksonville, FL
904-391-5118

Osceola
Osceola County Admin. Bldg.
17 S Vernon Ave. CCC
Kissimmee, FL
407-932-2940

Lake
Community Ctr./Lower Level
520 Baker St.
Lake County, FL
904-383-4474

Palm Beach
Sizzler Restaurant
1990 S Military Trail
Lake Worth, FL
407-694-0521

Lakeland
Citrus & Chemical Bank
114 N Tennessee Ave.
Lakeland, FL
813-644-0138

Harbor City
Melbourne Public Library
540 E Fee St.
Melbourne, FL
407-984-4316

Merritt Moonliter
777 E Merritt Island
Merritt Island, FL
407-453-3319

Merritt Island
Premier Cruise Lines
400 Challenger Rd.
Merritt Island, FL
407-452-4995

Miami Downtown
YMCA - World Trade Ctr.
90 SW 8th St., 3rd Fl.
Miami, FL
305-532-4327

Naples
Collier Govt. Complex
3301 E Tamiami/Bldg. F
Naples, FL
813-591-2700

Beaches Area
Seafood Galore
1589 Atlantic Blvd.
Neptune Beach, FL
904-241-0595

Gulf Breeze
Unity of Port Richey
5844 Pinehill Dr.
New Port Richey, FL
813-856-7964

North Miami Beach
McDonalds Senior Ctr.
17051 NE 19 Ave.
North Miami Beach, FL
305-895-2885

Triple Crown
McPherson Complex
County Commission Bldg.
Ocala, FL
904-854-0967

Orange Park
Hanley's Restaurant
1520 Park Ave.
Orange Park, FL
904-272-2268

Howard Rybolt
First Presbyterian Church
106 E Church St.
Orlando, FL
407-363-9892

Orlando Conquerors
Lee's Lakeside Rest.
431 E Central Blvd.
Orlando, FL
407-657-7129

Palatka
Palatka Mall
400 Highway 19
Palatka, FL
904-328-4718

Jupiter/Tequesta
Brighton Gardens
U.S. 1
Palm Beach Gardens, FL
407-286-2147

St. Petersburg
Chi-Chi's Restaurant
4020 Park Blvd.
Pinellas Park, FL
813-541-8573

Plantation
Universal Medical Ctr.
6701 W Sunrise Blvd.
Plantation, FL
305-764-8314

Pompano Beach
Denny's Restaurant
2671 N Federal Hwy.
Pompano Beach, FL
407-482-4522

Charlotte County
Punta Gorda Women's Club
118 Sullivan St.
Punta Gorda, FL
813-627-0724

Gold Coast
Olive Garden Restaurant
801 U.S. Hwy. 1
Riviera Beach, FL
407-848-2770

Daybreakers
Christo's Restaurant
107 W 1st St.
Sanford, FL
407-678-9584

Sarasota
Mel-O-Dee Restaurant
4685 N Tamiami Trail
Sarasota, FL
813-924-7756

AIA Toastmasters of South
   Brevard
Village Inn Restaurant
1190 Highway AIA
Satellite Beach, FL
407-773-0137

Golden Gulf
Florida Power Corp.
3201 34th St. S
St. Petersburg, FL
813-866-4432

Treasure Coast
500 Johnson Ave.
Stuart, FL
407-286-2147

Tallahassee
Hayden Burns Bldg.
605 Suwannee St. Rm. 350
Tallahassee, FL
904-891-8432

Seminole
Tallahassee Ford
243 N Magnolia Dr.
Tallahassee, FL
904-942-7307

Suncoast
Morrison's Cafeteria
11810 N Dale Mabry Hwy.
Tampa, FL
813-960-1010

Titusville
Denny's
3500 Cheney Hwy.
Titusville, FL
407-383-9069

Winter Park
Langford Hotel
300 E New England Ave.
Winter Park, FL
407-841-9452

Georgia

Albany
Elks Club
North Slappey Blvd.
Albany, GA
912-776-6414

Peachtree 25th
Peachtree - 25th Bldg.
1720 Peachtree Rd. NW
Atlanta, GA
404-347-5264

Alpharetta
Alpharetta North Park
Cogburn Rd.
Alpharetta, GA
404-740-9820

Buckhead
Calvin Court Apts.
479 E Paces Ferry Rd.
Atlanta, GA
404-299-5010

Classic City
Campus View Church of Christ
1360 S Lumpkin
Athens, GA
706-548-4811

Marietta Tower
Shoney's Restaurant
1445 N Expressway
Atlanta, GA
404-227-6805

Christopher
Morrison's Cafeteria
1544 Piedmont Ave.
Atlanta, GA
404-458-0865

Dogwood
Morrison's Cafeteria
N Druid HLS Rd. at I-85
Atlanta, GA
404-925-4004

Georgia State
GSU Student Ctr. Rm. 206
400 University Plaza
Atlanta, GA
404-469-6469

PB/T
Marta Hdqtrs., Suite 300
2424 Piedmont Rd. NE
Atlanta, GA
404-848-5740

Progressive
Holiday Inn Crown Plaza
4255 Ashford Dunwoody
Atlanta, GA
404-640-1333

Augusta
Shoney's Restaurant
3156 Wrightsboro Rd.
Augusta, GA
706-860-7889

Georgia-Carolina
The Green Jacket Restaurant
2567 Washington Rd.
Augusta, GA
706-724-0851

Clayton County
Unity Church P.O. Box 2180
7483 Mt. Zion Blvd.
Clayton County, GA
404-603-9016

Utoy
Red Oak United Methodist
   Church
3611 Roosevelt Hwy.
College Park, GA
404-461-8081

Columbus Uptown
Uptown on 1st
1039 1st Ave.
Columbus, GA
706-323-2437

Conyers-Rockdale
Boys and Girls Club
1015 O'Kelly St.
Conyers, GA
404-922-3809

Carpet Capital
Volunteer Action Center
Selvidge St.
Dalton, GA
706-226-8318

Decatur Communicators
Shoney's Restaurant
1849 Lawrenceville Hwy.
Decatur, GA
404-373-5930

Nightowl Revenooers
Internal Revenue Service
4800 Buford Hwy.
Doraville, GA
404-455-2029

Coffee
South Georgia College
Douglas, GA
912-384-8137

Alpha
County Line Methodist Church
4031 Old River Rd.
Ellenwood, GA
404-289-9313

Fort Valley
Fort Valley State College
213 Persons St.
Fort Valley, GA
912-825-1933

Gainesville
Shoney's Restaurant
Jesse Jewell Pkwy.
Gainesville, GA
404-532-9131

Kennesaw College
Shoney's Restaurant
Town Center Mall
Kennesaw, GA
404-436-0253

Macon
Medical Center of Middle GA
777 Hemlock St.
Macon, GA
912-474-8581

Charter Pride
Charter Lake Hospital
Education Center
3500 Riverside Dr.
Macon, GA
912-935-8238

Polk Street Speakers
St. James Episcopal Church
161 Church St.
Marietta, GA
404-953-1325

Gaveliers
National Tree Seed Lab
5156 Riggins Mill Rd.
Milledgeville, GA
912-751-3534

Monroe
Monroe-Walton County Library
217 W Spring St.
Monroe, GA
404-267-7583

President's Club
Georgia Pacific
2351 Button Gwinnett
Norcross, GA
404-978-8922

Northeast
Shoney's Restaurant
5905 Jimmy Carter Blvd.
Norcross, GA
404-441-7972

Horizon
Picadilly Cafeteria
3400 Holcomb Bridge
Norcross, GA
404-447-5372

Old Crocodiles
Roberta, GA
205-852-9175

Rome
Wstrn. Sizzlin Steak HS
801 Martha Berry Blvd.
Rome, GA
706-232-3452

Sandy Springs
Campbell Stone North
350 Carpenter Dr. NE
Sandy Springs, GA
404-392-9350

Savannah
Memorial Medical Center
4700 Waters Ave.
Savannah, GA
912-369-3238

Brunswick
Rich Seapak Shrimp Sch.
Airport Rd./St. Simons I
St. Simons Island, GA
912-634-1605

Stone Mountain
Safeco Ins. Company
1551 Juliette Rd.
Stone Mountain, GA
404-979-3832

Gwinnett
Matthews Cafeteria
2299 Main St.
Tucker, GA
404-925-2349

Illinois

Pride of the Fox
Mercy Center Hospital
1325 N Highland
Aurora, IL
708-232-4967

Broadview 3303
Broadview Village Hall
2350 S 25th Ave.
Broadville, IL
708-484-7736

Speakers Forum
Railroad Retirement Brd.Bldg.
844 N Rush St.
Chicago, IL
312-984-2218

Communicators
Advance Bk, Lower Level
9730 S Western Ave.
Chicago, IL
312-779-1892

South Shore
South Shore Public Library
2500 E 73rd St.
Chicago, IL
312-436-7072

Silvertones
AT & T Corporate Center
227 W Monroe - 4th Fl.
Chicago, IL
312-353-8747

Quaker Toastmasters of
    Chicago
Quaker Conference Rm.
321 N Clark St.
Chicago, IL
312-222-6811

Triad
Kennedy King College
6800 S Wentworth Ave.
Chicago, IL
708-332-1060

Chicago Heights
The Egg & I Restaurant
Vollmer Rd. & Dixie Hwy.
Chicago Heights, IL
708-503-1248

Deerbrook Park
Deerfield Public Library
920 Waukegan Rd.
Deerfield, IL
708-940-1839

Des Plaines
Des Plaines Public Library
841 Graceland
Des Plaines, IL
708-635-6351

Ellsworth Park Toastmasters
2400 Curtis St.
Downers Grove, IL
708-985-4774

Northwest
Elk Grove Village Hall
901 Wellington Ave.
Elk Grove, IL
708-437-4474

Elmhurst
Messiah Lutheran Church
130 W Butterfield Rd.
Elmhurst, IL
708-279-2724

Town Criers
Glenellyn Civic Center
535 Duane St.
Glen Ellyn, IL
708-682-3662

North Suburban
Glenview Public Library
1930 Glenview Rd.
Glenview, IL
708-577-3698

Homewood-Flossmoor
Grand Prairie Library
3479 W 183rd St.
Hazel Crest, IL
708-747-9364

Hinsdale
Hinsdale Public Library
20 E. Maple
Hinsdale, IL
708-579-9337

West Suburban
Lagrange Park Library
555 N Lagrange Rd.
La Grange, IL
708-354-5458

Alpine
Harry Kniggee Center
99 E Main St.
Lake Zurich, IL
708-526-4169

Daniel Wright
Lamb's Farm Country Inn
Rt. 176 & I-94
Libertyville, IL
708-680-7006

Comm. Christians
Brandywine Club House
1 South 130 Ardmore
Lombard, IL
708-682-3662

Long Grove
Kemper Insurance Co.
1 Kemper Dr. Rm. 1C
Long Grove, IL
708-230-2254

Niles Township
Morton Grove Library
6140 Lincoln Ave.
Morton Grove, IL
312-743-7453

Mount Prospect
South Church
501 S Emerson St.
Mount Prospect, IL
708-632-0660

Naperville
Wesley United Methodist
  Church
21 E Franklin
Naperville, IL
708-355-4580

The Indian Hill
AT & T Bell Labs
2000 North Naperville
Naperville, IL
708-979-0743

Strowger
AG Communication System
  Corp.
400 N Wolf Rd.
Northlake, IL
708-681-7131

Oak Brook
Drake Office Plaza
2211 York Rd. # 204
Oak Brook, IL
708-832-7100

Oak Forest
Acorn Public Library
15624 S Central
Oak Forest, IL
312-881-1112

Oak Park
Maze Library
834 Gunderson
Oak Park, IL
708-771-0567

Orland Park
First Chicago Bank 2nd Fl.
151 St. & La Grange Rd.
Orland Park, IL
708-460-5210

Palatine
Palatine Library
700 N North Court
Palatine, IL
708-397-1177

Park Forest
Freedom Hall
4120 Lakewood Blvd.
Park Forest, IL
708-747-5198

Park Ridge
1st United Methodist Church
418 Touhy Ave. 3rd Fl.
Park Ridge, IL
708-965-7512

Arlington Heights
Rolling Meadows Library
3110 Martin Lane
Rolling Meadows, IL
708-706-4000

Northwest Suburban
Motorola Inc.
1303 E Algonquin Rd.
Schaumburg, IL
708-632-3267

Schaumburg Area
Woodfield Corporate Center
425 N Martingale
Schaumburg, IL
708-885-3573

Skokie
Skokie Village Hall
5127 Oakton Avenue
Skokie, IL
312-631-9146

Happy Toasters
Mayer Kaplan JCC
5050 W Church St.
Skokie, IL
708-679-6630

Community
Holy Family Ambulatory
   Center
201 E Strong
Wheeling, IL
708-949-1810

Woodridge
United Methodist Church
2700 75th St.
Woodridge, IL
708-963-6961

Louisiana

Greater Bossier
Morrison's Cafeteria
2323 Old Minden Rd.
Bossier City, LA
318-741-8824

Red River Early Bird
Shoney's Restaurant
Youree Dr.
Shreveport, LA
318-687-4149

Shreveport
Shreve Memorial Library
424 Texas St.
Shreveport, LA
318-742-3619

Massachusetts

Isaac Davis
Raymond Grey J H S
Charter Rd.
Acton, MA
505-456-8203

John Alden
Chamber Of Commerce
859 Massachusetts Ave.
Boston, MA
800-222-5860

Researchers
Base Commander's Conf.
Rm. 1600/Rm. 217 Bldg. 1630
Bedford, MA
508-872-1625

Brockton
West Side Public Library
540 Forest Ave.
Brockton, MA
508-587-8827

Boston
Boston University
  Communication School
640 Commonwealth Ave.
Boston, MA
617-567-7644

Chelmsford
Old Chelmsford Town Hall
Rt. 4 North Rd.
Chelmsford, MA
508-256-3775

Alcott
Concord Public Library
Main St.
Concord, MA
508-369-6934

Merrimack
Prescott House
140 Prescott St.
Lawrence, MA
508-373-1064

Achievers
South Shore Bank
Copeland Dr.
Mansfield, MA
508-226-0238

Speech Invaders
Waters Div./Millipore
34 Maple St.
Milford, MA
508-478-7770

Framingham/Natick
Morse Inst./Natick Lib.
14 E Central St.
Natick, MA
508-626-2776

Boston West
First Parish Unitarian Church
23 Dedham St.
Needham, MA
617-964-5040

Whaling City
Ronnie's Seafood Rest.
804 Belleville Ave.
New Bedford, MA
508-979-3405

Quincy
Fore River Club
16 Nevada Rd.
Quincy, MA
617-472-9479

Eastern Middlesex
Stoneham Public Library
431 Main St.
Stoneham, MA
617-396-7847

Northshore
First Baptist Church
159 Lowell St.
Swampscott, MA
508-927-8362

Minutemen
Hill American Legion Post #15
215 Waverly Oaks Rd.
Waltham, MA
617-232-1477

Cape Cod
Cape Cod Community College
Rt. 132
West Barnstable, MA
508-428-5032

Central
James Street Restaurant
70 James St.
Worcester, MA
508-753-5031

Michigan

Cereal City
Shrank's Cafeteria
85 W Michigan
Battle Creek, MI
800-334-7924

Greater Flint
YMCA
411 E 3rd. St.
Flint, MI
313-238-8366

Early Bird
Waters Building
Basement Conference Room
Grand Rapids, MI
616-874-9082

Jackson
Jackson Main Library
244 W Michigan Ave.
Jackson, MI
517-787-2300

Strictly Speaking
The Upjohn Co., Bldg. 298
7000 Portage Rd.
Kalamazoo, MI
616-323-4605

The Oldsmobile
General Motors
920 Townsend St.
Lansing, MI
517-377-6185

Tittabawassee
Midland Public School Admin.
600 E Carpenter
Midland, MI
517-835-7116

Midland
Northwood University
NADA Ctr./3225 Cook Rd.
Midland, MI
517-835-7116

Breakfast
Cherokee Restaurant
Sherman Blvd.
Muskegon, MI
616-842-7271

Hi-Noon
Zimmer's
3812 Pine Grove Ave.
Port Huron, MI
313-985-4592

Harvey Spaulding YMCA
Saginaw YMCA
1915 Fordney
Saginaw, MI
517-791-1121

Lock City
Dept. of Social Studies
208 Bingham
Sault Ste. Marie, MI
705-253-8764

Main Street
St. Joseph Public Library
500 Market St.
St. Joseph, MI
616-428-4563

Cherry Capital
Grand Traverse Mall
3200 S Airport Rd. W
Traverse City, MI
616-946-7483

New Jersey

Bergen
Bogota Recreation Ctr.
PO Box 101-162 Main St.
Bogota, NJ
201-343-2647

Clifton
Staceys Restaurant
615 Van Houten Ave.
Clifton, NJ
201-783-4708

Elmwood Park
Holiday Inn Conference Ctr.
Elmwood Park, NJ
201-963-0022

Holmdel Speakers
AT&T Holmdel Location
Red Hill Location
Holmdel, NJ
908-834-1245

Woodbridge
Iselin Public Library
1081 Green St.
Iselin, NJ
908-634-0251

We Search
Schering-Plough Corp.
2015 Galloping Hill Rd.
Kenilworth, NJ
908-298-7269

Midland Park
Ramsey Public Library
30 Wyckoff Ave.
Midland Park, NJ
201-337-5496

Madison Avenue Tigers
Madison Public Library
39 Keep St.
Morristown, NJ
201-984-9115

Mutual Benefit Life
Mutual Benefit Life Co.
520 Broad St.
Newark, NJ
201-481-8325

Speakatway
AT&T, Room C50-52A38
30 Knightsbridge Rd.
Piscataway, NJ
908-885-6525

Ridgewood
Pease Library
30 Garber Square
Ridgewood, NJ
201-934-7440

Fairleigh Early Birds
FDU Student Union Bldg.
223 Montross Ave.
Rutherford, NJ
201-939-0939

Somerville
Somerset County Library
N. Bridge St. & Vogt Dr.
Somerville, NJ
201-587-0090

Summit
Hoescht-Celanese Labs
86 Morris Avenue
Summit, NJ
201-376-8637

Wayne
Wayne Valley High School
551 Valley Rd.
Wayne, NJ
201-628-2613

Toastmasters of Westfield
1st Savings/Scotch Plains
Fanwood Train Station
Westfield, NJ
908-889-1890

New York

Talk of the Town
Lutheran Chr/Messiah
42-15 165th St.
Flushing, NY
718-462-8509

Freeport-Hempstead
Freeport Memorial Library
114 W Merrick Rd.
Freeport, NY
516-466-8057

Huntington
Walt Whitman High School
W Hills Rd., Forum Rm.
Huntington, NY
516-754-8691

Knickerbocker
Church Of The Covenant
310 E 42nd St.
New York, NY
212-752-7204

Graybar
7th Regiment Armory
643 Park Ave.
New York, NY
718-937-7380

Vanderbilt
North American Philips
100 E 42nd St.
New York, NY
212-850-5540

Equitable
Equitable Tower
787 7th Ave.
New York, NY
212-554-2709

Toastmasters 21 Club
21st Fl., DD's Conf. Rm.
50 Murray St.
New York, NY
212-264-8692

Bryant Park
Amer. Standard/Grace Bldg.
1114 6th Ave., 19th Fl.
New York, NY
212-512-1402

Readers Digest
Readers Digest-Pegasus Rm.
Reader's Digest Rd.
Pleasantville, NY
914-238-5872

Westchester
Leo Mintzer Comm. Ctr.
Underhill St.
Purchase, NY
212-370-1144

Roosevelt Island
Rivercross Upper Community Rm.
531 Main St.
Roosevelt Island, NY
212-355-4243

Northern Brookhaven
Suffolk County Community College
Nichols Rd.
Selden, NY
516-878-4648

Richmond County
Staten Island University Hospital
242 Mason Place
Staten Island, NY
718-987-1339

Ohio

Opportunity Park
Uniroyal-Goodrich Co.
600 South Main St.
Akron, OH
216-733-0337

Downtown
Akron City Club
50 S Main St.
Akron, OH
216-379-4753

Alliance
Don Pancho's Restaurant
9 S Union Ave.
Alliance, OH
216-823-0792

Buckeye Advanced
Beachwood Library
25501 Shaker
Beachwood, OH
216-765-1711

Pleasant Valley
Cuyahoga County Library
4480 Ridge Rd.
Brooklyn, OH
216-741-2193

Towne Club 443
Stark Technical College
6200 Frank Rd. NW
Canton, OH
216-494-2210

Chagrin Valley
Chagrin Falls Library
100 E Orange St.
Chagrin Falls, OH
216-247-7493

Cleveland
Illuminating Co.
Behind 55 Pub Square
Cleveland, OH
216-689-9732

Forest City
Diocese/Cleveland Office Bldg.
1031 Superior Ave.
Cleveland, OH
216-621-9181

Akron
Country Manor Restaurant
1886 State Rd.
Cuyahoga Falls, OH
216-867-5245

Summit
Country Manor Restaurant
1886 State Rd.
Cuyahoga Falls, OH
216-836-4787

High Noon
Argo-Tech Corp.
23555 Euclid Ave.
Euclid, OH
216-692-6230

Village
Maple Hights Public Library
5225 Library Lane
Garfield Heights, OH
216-467-9675

Midway
Midway 953
118 Yorkshire Ct.
Lorain, OH
216-365-9379

Western Reserve
The Old Tavern
South Ridge Rd.
Madison, OH
216-428-9121

Mansfield
Park Place Hotel
191 Park Ave W/Pk E Rm.
Mansfield, OH
419-938-3523

Marion
Big Boy Family Restaurant
1833 Marion-Mt Gilead
Marion, OH
614-387-1091

Medina
Best Western Motel
Rt. 18 & I-71
Medina, OH
216-725-6997

Lake
Mentor Methodist Church
800 Mentor Ave.
Mentor, OH
216-224-1234

Berea
Briarcliff Party Center
7618 Pearl Rd.
Middleburg Heights, OH
216-398-6156

Mount Vernon
Mt. Vernon Public Library
Mulberry & Sugar St.
Mount Vernon, OH
614-694-6007

Nordonia Gaveliers
N/Field Multi-Serv. Ctr.
9370 Olde 8 Rd. Rm. 203
Northfield, OH
216-838-5076

Diamond
First Church of Christ
422 Mentor Ave.
Painesville, OH
216-352-4858

West Side
King Wah Restaurant
20668 Center Ridge Rd.
Rocky River, OH
216-371-4434

Shelby
Ikes Family Restaurant
Mansfield Ave.
Shelby, OH
419-342-6948

Lunchtime Linguists
Brown Derby Restaurant
4910 Northfield Rd.
Warrensville Hights, OH
216-642-7509

Bailey Toastmasters
Willowick Civic Center
900 Worden Rd.
Wickliffe, OH
216-944-6598

That's Easy
Holiday Inn-Lilies Rest.
28500 Euclid Ave.
Willoughby, OH
216-946-8772

Wayne County
Wayne County Public Library
304 N Market St.
Wooster, OH
216-262-6823

Oregon

Astoria
Andrew & Steve's Cafe
1196 Marine Dr.
Astoria, OR
503-325-3945

Cedar Hills
Elmer's Pancake House
Cedar Hills Blvd.
Beaverton, OR
503-648-8721

Bend Morning
Gandy Dancer Restaurant
Scandia Plaza Hwy. 97
Bend, OR
503-388-4332

Canby
Cottage Kitchen
314 NW 1st Ave.
Canby, OR
503-651-3480

Corvallis
Towne House
350 SW 4th
Corvallis, OR
503-752-0342

Eugene
King's Table
2470 W 11th
Eugene, OR
503-344-9292

Yawn Patrol
Country Steaks & Cakes
9th & Garfield
Eugene, OR
503-461-3518

Grants Pass
Josephine Cnty. Court House
6th St. (Btwn. A & B St.)
Grants Pass, OR
503-474-2763

Gresham
Elmers Pancake & Steak
  House
1555 E Burnside
Gresham, OR
503-665-9815

Hillsboro
Millers Homestead Inn
640 SE 10th Ave.
Hillsboro, OR
503-357-7683

Bootstrappers
Chelsea's Restaurant
2425 Lancaster Dr. NE
Keizer, OR
503-390-0852

MODOC
JR's Family Restaurant
2322 Washburn Way
Klamath Falls, OR
503-882-2741

Lake Oswego
United Church of Christ
1111 Country Club Rd.
Lake Oswego, OR
503-620-2741

Jackson
Kopper Kitchen
1150 Barnett Rd.
Medford, OR
503-779-2971

Milwaukie
Monarch Hotel
12566 SE 93rd
Milwaukie, OR
503-235-7827

Mid
J's Restaurant
220 N Pacific Hwy.
Monmouth, OR
503-371-3239

Newberg
Horseless Carriage Restaurant
607 E First
Newberg, OR
503-590-1662

Coast Toasties
Embarcadero
1000 SE Bay Blvd.
Newport, OR
503-265-6356

Portland
Village Inn
1621 NE 10th
Portland, OR
503-635-4576

Oregon
Portland Hilton Downtown
921 SW 6th Ave.
Portland, OR
503-275-6650

Oregon Trail
Federal Bldg. Cafeteria
1220 SW 3rd. Ave.
Portland, OR
503-292-0076

S. M. Chanticleers
NW Natural Gas Bldg.
220 NW 2nd Ave.
Portland, OR
503-226-4211

First Masters
Standard Ins. Plaza
1100 SW 6th - 3rd Fl.
Portland, OR
503-225-2145

Electric Toasters
World Trade Center
121 SW Salmon St.
Portland, OR
503-464-8197

Noontime
Auditorium - 2nd Fl.
920 SW 6th Ave.
Portland, OR
503-464-6187

Advisors
Ross Island Center
Portland Comm. College
Portland, OR
503-295-2944

Tabor Toastmasters
Fred Meyer-Eves Rest.
39th & SE Hawthorne
Portland, OR
503-232-1584

Roseburg
Tom Tom Restaurant
65 Garden Valley Shopping
    Ctr.
Roseburg, OR
503-673-0237

Salem
Denny's Restaurant
3155 Ryan Dr. SE
Salem, OR
503-581-7056

Executive
Executive Bldg., Conf. Rm. A
155 Cottage NE
Salem, OR
503-363-4611

High Noon
Oregon Dept. of Revenue
955 Center St. NE
Salem, OR
503-945-6550

Springfield
Wild Plum Restaurant
1537 Mohawk Blvd.
Springfield, OR
503-726-2057

Stayton
Stayton Coop. Tele. Co. Whs.
Brd. Rm. 475 N Second
Stayton, OR
503-399-7079

Wallmasters International
Old Country Buffet
13500 SW Pacific Hwy.
Tigard, OR
503-590-0928

Tillamook
Shilo Restaurant
2535 Main St.
Tillamook, OR
503-842-8285

New Horizons
Pegasus Bldg.
30250 SW Parkway #1
Wilsonville, OR
503-682-5802

Rhode Island

Providence
Regency Plaza
60 Broadway
Providence, RI
401-331-1644

Ocean State
Super Stop & Shop
300 Quaker Lane, Rt. 2
Warwick, RI
401-397-6843

Texas

Metrocrest Toastmasters
Anne Maries Kitchen
5290 Belt Line Rd. #116
Addison, TX
214-335-3741

CPA
L'l Walnut Creek Br. Library
835 E Rundberg Lane
Austin, TX
512-445-6670

Arlington
Iron Skillet Restaurant
I-20 at Matlock
Arlington, TX
817-860-9544

Texas
Wyatts Cafeteria
Hancock Shopping Ctr.
Austin, TX
512-458-5831

Athens
Best Western Inn
Highway 31
Athens, TX
903-675-1267

Aim High
TDMHMR Central Office
909 W 45th St., Rm. 240
Austin, TX
512-450-4529

Pecan Valley
Red Wagon Restaurant
401 N Main
Brownwood, TX
915-643-4941

Silver Tongue
College Station Conf. Ctr.
1300 George Bush Dr.
Bryan College Station, TX
409-775-7506

Burkburnett
Circle H. Barbeque
301 S Berry
Burkburnett, TX
817-569-2509

Aggie Toasters
Rudder Tower
Texas A&M University
College Station, TX
406-823-4512

Corpus Christi
Shoney's Rest.
Spid at Staples
Corpus Christi, TX
512-241-7082

The Big D
The Doubletree Inn
8250 N Central Expwy.
Dallas, TX
817-540-5562

Greater Dallas
Park Cities Inn
6101 Hillcrest Ave.
Dallas, TX
214-497-9525

Trinity Toastmasters
JoJo's Restaurant
6232 E Mockingbird Lane
Dallas, TX
214-821-9738

Metro-Speakers
JoJo's Restaurant
12909 Midway Rd. at LBJ
Dallas, TX
214-234-4973

Whiterock
Denny's Restaurant
10433 S Central Expwy.
Dallas, TX
214-238-5471

Toast of The Town
Nations Bk. Elm Bk. Ctr.
1401 Elm St. 9th Fl.
Dallas, TX
214-978-0466

Golden Triangle
GTE Directories Corp.
1 W Airfield Dr.
Dallas/Ft. Worth Apt., TX
214-453-7362

Wise County
Church of Christ
608 N Trinity
Decatur, TX
817-627-5153

Denton Toastmasters
Lake Forest Good Samaritan
3901 Montecito
Denton, TX
817-382-6199

Red Bird
Mama Jo's Restaurant
615 N Hampton Rd.
Desoto, TX
214-224-8635

Lonestar
Killeen Comm. Ctr.
2201 E Bus. Hwy. 190
Fort Hood, TX
817-526-9495

Plus-Two
TCOM Bldg. 3 Rm. 110
3500 Camp Bowie Blvd.
Fort Worth, TX
817-293-0754

Cowtown
Old South Pancake House
1507 S University Dr.
Fort Worth, TX
817-926-8814

Reveille
Old South Pancake House
1507 S University Dr.
Ft. Worth, TX
817-337-3612

Ridglea
Old South Pancake House
1307 University Dr.
Ft. Worth, TX
817-370-2467

Anico Articulators
Anico Exec. Dining Room
1 Moody Plaza 19th Fl.
Galveston, TX
409-763-1112

Garland
International House of
    Pancakes
1313 W Centerville Rd.
Garland, TX
214-613-9348

Harlingen
Dolly Vincent Hospital
400 E Hwy. 77 Board Rm.
Harlingen, TX
210-399-4767

High Noon
Downtown YMCA
1600 Louisiana
Houston, TX
713-654-7665

Spaceland
House of Prayer Lutheran
1515 Bay Area Blvd.
Houston, TX
713-483-6803

Daybreakers
La Quinta Motor Inn
4015 SW Frwy. at Wesleyan
Houston, TX
713-664-0475

Magic Circle
Rice Epicurean 2nd Fl.
San Felipe at Voss
Houston, TX
713-662-8201

Lone Star Speakers
Memorial Hospital Cafeteria
7600 Beechnut
Houston, TX
713-980-4075

Jawbreakers
Town & Country Mall
Comm. Rm.
12600 Katy Frwy.
Houston, TX
713-497-7305

Tower
Texas Commerce Bank Tower
Travis St. 50th Fl.
Houston, TX
713-821-1541

Talk of the Town
Holiday Inn West
I-10 at Hwy. 6
Houston, TX
713-496-5137

Texas Avenue
The Houston Chronicle
801 Texas Ave., 4th Fl.
Houston, TX
713-220-7467

Humble Opinion
Steak & Ale Restaurant
19707 Hwy. 59 N
Humble, TX
713-548-4577

Mid Cities
Hoffbrau Steakhouse
Airport Freeway
Hurst, TX
817-498-6511

Mid-Cities
Hoffbrau Restaurant
1833 W Airport Freeway
Hurst, TX
817-498-0840

Oration Plus
Computer Assoc., Rm. 1424B
909 E Las Colinas Blvd.
Irving, TX
214-556-7671

Irving
Crystal's Pizza
930 W Airport Freeway
Irving, TX
214-986-1345

Katy Toastmasters
Epiphanny Church
1520 Norwalk
Katy, TX
713-550-3634

Lewisville
Banquet Rm., Point N Rest
Garden Ridge Blvd. &
Main St.
Lewisville, TX
214-317-1326

Rise & Shine Toasters
Hot Bisquit Restaurant
Loop 281 & Gilmer Rd.
Longview, TX
903-757-7575

Nacogdoches
Cappelli's Restaurant
3303 North St.
Nacogdoches, TX
409-560-9201

New Braunfels
Summit Center
2405 IH 35 West
New Braunfels, TX
210-379-4865

Plano Frontier
MCI Corp.
2400 N Glenville
Plano, TX
214-918-7099

Richardson
Holiday Inn
1655 N Central Expwy.
Richardson, TX
214-240-0214

Fort Bend
George Memorial Library
1001 Golfview Dr.
Richmond, TX
713-265-8631

Hilltop
NCO Club Annex
Kelly AFB
San Antonio, TX
210-977-2546

Business-Professional
La Quinta Motor Inn
333 NE Loop 410
San Antonio, TX
210-492-0375

Texoma Toastmasters
Shoneys Restaurant
Texoma Pkwy.
Sherman, TX
903-463-1832

Greater Tyler
Shoney's Restaurant
3701 Troup Hwy.
Tyler, TX
903-534-0088

Tyler
Sweet Sue's Restaurant
3350 S SW Loop 323
Tyler, TX
903-566-7510

Waco Tale Twisters
VA Regional Office
1400 N Valley Mills Dr.
Waco, TX
817-776-6436

Clear Lake
Mario's Flying Pizza
618 Nasa Rd. 1
Webster, TX
713-333-3934

Wichita Falls
Luby's Cafeteria
1801 9th St.
Wichita Falls, TX
817-723-0761

Virginia

Milpercen
Hoffman Bldg. II
200 Stovall St., Rm. 7N20
Alexandria, VA
703-325-0516

AMCATS
A.M.C. Bldg.
5001 Eisenhower Ave.
Alexandria, VA
703-274-5540

Annandale
J.C. Presbyterian Church
6531 Columbia Pike
Annandale, VA
703-569-9564

Anchor
National Center Z
2521 Jefferson Davis
Arlington, VA
703-548-7994

Challenger Toastmasters
Le Peep Restaurant
2300 Clarendon Blvd.
Arlington, VA
703-256-2890

Helmsmen
Executive Dining Room
Rm. 3C1060
Pentagon
Arlington, VA
703-614-0665

Generally Speaking
Crystal Mall #3, Rm. 316
1931 Jeff Davis Hwy.
Crystal City, VA
703-305-7577

Fairfax
Fairfax High School
3500 Old Lee Hwy.
Fairfax, VA
703-573-1764

Old Dominion
Hazel-Peterson Board Room
12701 Fairlakes Circle 4F
Fairfax, VA
703-978-3208

Lucky
Office/Hearings & Appeals
5701 Leesburg Pike #1506
Falls Church, VA
703-305-0286

Gladiators
NASSIF Bldg. Rm. 714/318
5611 Columbia Pike
Falls Church, VA
703-756-1242

Nova
Falls Church High School
7521 Jaguar Trail
Falls Church, VA
703-255-0420

Reston-Herndon Toastmasters
Reston Regional Library
11900 Bowman Towne Dr.
Reston, VA
703-471-7820

Springfield
Versar Corp. Conf. Rm.
6850 Versar Center
Springfield, VA
703-451-7107

Vienna
Vienna Community Ctr.
120 Cherry St. SE
Vienna, VA
703-938-1899

Washington

Harbor
Wishkah Cookhouse
500 W Wishkah Ave.
Aberdeen, WA
206-249-4334

Auburn
Chandelle's Restaurant
333 15th St. NE
Auburn, WA
206-854-4766

Bellevue East Side
Angelo's Restaurant
1830-130th Ave. NE
Bellevue, WA
206-649-8457

Overlake
Paccar Bldg., Mt. Ranier Rm.
  777
106 NE Basement
Bellevue, WA
206-455-5850

Bellingham
West One Bank
121 W Holly St.
Bellingham, WA
206-354-0836

Bellingham
Salvation Army Bldg.
2912 Northwest Ave.
Bellingham, WA
206-734-5378

Bremerton
Kitsap Lake Baptist Church
5802 Wilmont
Bremerton, WA
206-692-2427

Leading Knights
Burien Elks # 2143
14006 1st. Ave. South
Burien, WA
206-246-1933

Chehalis-Centralia
Peppermill Restaurant
1232 Alder
Chehalis, WA
206-262-3164

Everett
Village by the Lake
820 Cady Rd. Cabana
Everett, WA
206-353-6855

Mun-E-Men
Everett Pacific Hotel
3105 Pine St.
Everett, WA
206-338-0579

Early Opinions
Evergreen Branch Library
9512 Evergreen Way
Everett, WA
206-252-9773

Town Criers
Federal Way Comm. Ctr.
33901 9th Ave. S
Federal Way, WA
206-839-5042

Fort Lewis
American Lake Club
North Fort Lewis
Fort Lewis, WA
206-756-6825

Peninsula
Gig Harbor Chamber of
Commerce
3125 Judson
Gig Harbor, WA
206-564-2399

Green River
Denny's Restaurant
1246 N Central
Kent, WA
206-432-8433

Kirkland Eclectics
Kirkland Congregational
   Church
106 5th Ave.
Kirkland, WA
206-882-1645

Meridian
First Community Bank
721 College St. SE
Lacey, WA
206-586-8436

Early Words
Fergusons Restaurant
729 Ocean Beach Hwy.
Longview, WA
206-578-3834

Lynden
Fairway Cafe
1726 Front St.
Lynden, WA
206-366-3671

Lynwood Lunchmasters
Azteca Restaurant
Alderwood Mall Blvd.
Lynnwood, WA
206-355-6917

Mount Vernon
Mount Vernon Elks Lodge
2111 Riverside Dr.
Mount Vernon, WA
206-428-0142

Alliant Techsystems
6500 Harbour Hts. Pky.
Mukilteo, WA
206-356-3731

Oak Harbor
VFW Hall
3037 N Goldie Rd.
Oak Harbor, WA
206-675-5367

Olympia
Quality Inn Westwater
2300 Evergreen Dr.
Olympia, WA
206-943-2889

Port Angeles
Aggie's Restaurant
602 East Front St.
Port Angeles, WA
206-452-4216

Little Norway
N Kitsap High School
18360 Caldart Ave. NE
Poulsbo, WA
206-373-1539

Word Weavers
Mt. View Lutheran Church
3505 122nd Ave. E
Puyallup, WA
206-474-3043

Willows Voices
Rocket Research Co.
11441 Willows Rd. NE
Redmond, WA
206-885-5010

Sweptwing
Vince's Restaurant
2815 NE Sunset Blvd.
Renton, WA
206-575-0450

Seattle International
Seattle, WA
206-246-1345

Excel-O-Rators
National Oceanic Atmos
    Admin.
7600 Sand PT Way NE Bldg. 9
Seattle, WA
206-542-5963

Totem
Grove Restaurant/Grosvenor
500 Wall St.
Seattle, WA
206-774-1695

Pro Master
DPRO Conference Room
Boeing Bldg. 18-231
Seattle, WA
206-773-8922

The Red Barn
Joyce's Restaurant
9100 E Marginal Way S
Seattle, WA
206-641-3469

Shelton
Timbers Restaurant
N 7th & E Railroad Ave.
Shelton, WA
206-426-7475

Tacoma
Tacoma Public Library
7001 Sixth Ave.
Tacoma, WA
206-752-2480

Evergreen 333
Grazie Ristorante
2301 N 30th St.
Tacoma, WA
206-564-2399

Trinity
Trinity Lutheran Church
12115 Park Ave. S
Tacoma, WA
206-537-4842

Puget Prattlers
Fern Hill Library
765 S 84th St.
Tacoma, WA
206-752-3959

Eyeopeners
Cattin's Restaurant
7826 S Tacoma Way
Tacoma, WA
206-474-2842

Achievers
St. Clare Hospital
11315 Bridgeport Way
Tacoma, WA
206-474-2842

Southcenter
Andy's Tukwila Station
2408 West Valley Rd.
Tukwila, WA
206-630-3317

Vancouver
Mama's Bake Shop
708 78th St.
Vancouver, WA
206-687-0866

Totem Pole
Totem Pole Family Restaurant
7720 NE Hwy. 99
Vancouver, WA
206-576-1413

INDEX